Once Upon A Time

Once Upon A Time

Amy E. Dean

First published January, 1987.

ISBN: 0-89486-407-6

Printed in the United States of America.

Editor's Note:
  Hazelden Educational Materials offers a variety of information on
chemical dependency and related areas. Our publications do not
necessarily represent Hazelden or its programs, nor do they offi-
cially speak for any Twelve Step organization.

DEDICATION

To Margery . . . the beginning

TO ANY PARENT

(Adapted by the author from "To Any Dad," Author Unknown)

There are little eyes upon you, watching night and day;
There are little ears that quickly take in every word you say;
There are little hands all eager to do all things you do,
And a little child who's dreaming of the day to be like you.

You're the little child's idol, you're the wisest of the wise;
In the little mind about you no suspicions ever rise;
The child believes in you devoutly, and holds that all you do
The child will say and do in your way when grown up like you.

There's a wide-eyed little one who believes you're always right,
With ears always open, you're watched both day and night,
You are setting an example every day in all you do,
For the little child who's waiting to grow up just like you.

AUTHOR'S NOTE

In many of the following stories you may find reference made to the fourteen questions read at an Adult Children of Alcoholics meeting. These questions describe some of the characteristics felt by someone who grew up in an alcoholic environment. You may find you share a few, many, or all of these characteristics in your present life and personality.

1. Do I often feel isolated and afraid of people and authority figures?
2. Have I observed myself to be an approval seeker, losing my own identity in the process?
3. Do I feel overly frightened of angry people and personal criticism?
4. Do I often feel I'm a victim in personal and career relationships?
5. Do I sometimes feel I have an overdeveloped sense of responsibility, which makes it easier to be concerned with others rather than myself?
6. Do I find it hard to look at my own faults and my own responsibility to myself?
7. Do I get guilt feelings when I stand up for myself instead of giving in to others?
8. Do I feel addicted to excitement?
9. Do I confuse love with pity and tend to love people I can pity and rescue?
10. Do I find it hard to feel or express feelings, including feelings such as joy or happiness?
11. Do I find I judge myself harshly?
12. Do I have a low sense of self-esteem?
13. Do I often feel abandoned in the course of my relationships?
14. Do I tend to be a reactor, instead of an actor?

You may find the support of therapy and/or ACOA meetings beneficial in helping you deal with these characteristics.

ACKNOWLEDGMENTS

I would like to recognize the courage of each of the twenty people who shared their stories with me. I am grateful for the trust they had in me to accurately portray the struggles they have known since childhood.

I'd like to thank Hazelden Educational Materials and my editor, Monica Dwyer Abress, for their belief in the necessity of this book and its significance to the entire community of Adult Children of Alcoholics and those that interact with them.

Finally, I'd like to thank you — the reader — for having the courage to pick up this book. Perhaps you, too, will find your own story within these pages. May you then be able to find, through the help of the program, a future filled with freedom from your past.

INTRODUCTION

"It is absurd to think that life begins for us at birth. The pattern is set far back; we merely step into the process."

— Kathleen Coyle, Irish novelist

ONCE upon a time, a man and a woman met each other and fell in love. The man asked the woman to marry him. She said "yes." They had a wonderful wedding and a romantic honeymoon. They were happy. Soon they began to raise a family. Their kids grew up healthy and spent a great deal of quality time with their parents until they were older. Then they fell in love with the person of their dreams, got married, and raised a family. . . .

Wait!

Some childhood stories are filled with such joy and happiness. But other childhood stories are nowhere near the lovely simplicity of that fantasy story. They could be called fairy tales, but written by "the brothers grim." They are about childhoods in dysfunctional homes influenced by addictive diseases, mental illnesses, or emotional disorders. These childhoods know intimately times of sadness or pain; physical, verbal, or sexual abuse; separation or divorce; or foster homes and guardians. Most often, the disease of alcoholism is the primary cause of the dysfunction, although other addictions to food, drugs, work, and gambling can evoke the same destructive results.

Then why say these childhood stories are like fairy tales?

First, every fairy tale begins with, "Once upon a time. . . ," meaning the story had its roots in the past. So it is with people who reach adulthood after growing up in dysfunctional environments. Their roots are in the past memories of what it was like for them to grow up in their homes.

Second, each fairy tale has some major problem, difficulty, or tragedy that needs to be overcome. Cinderella had her horrible sisters. Snow White had the poisoned apple. The Three Little Pigs had the Big Bad Wolf. People who grew up in dysfunctional environments have to overcome the pain of the past and the negative messages they were given about themselves as children.

Finally, every fairy tale works out when the problem is overcome and the hero or heroine "lives happily ever after." When people who grew up in dysfunctional environments learn positive behaviors for themselves, they too can live happily ever after.

People who grew up in dysfunctional homes share a common fairy tale. The problem they need to overcome is the influence that the addiction or behaviors had on the lives of their parents, and ultimately, upon their own lives. From the parent to the child and, later, to the maturing adult, the effects of the dysfunctional home are passed on like family heirlooms.

This book can almost be seen as a collection of fairy tales. In each separate story, you'll read about someone's unhappy childhood and learn about the problems each person needed to overcome as he or she reached adulthood. You'll read of people's struggles to find themselves, then share in their happiness as they find ways to overcome their difficulties. Each story has its own balance of negatives and positives: disbelief and belief, doubt and faith, chaos and peace, stagnation and growth, hopelessness and hope.

A person who grows up in an alcoholic environment is called a child of an alcoholic (COA). An environment is alcoholic when it has been affected in some way by the alcoholism of a family member. There doesn't have to be visible drinking in order to qualify as an alcoholic environment. All it takes is an alcoholic somewhere in the family tree of either parent in order to have alcoholic behaviors passed down from one generation to the next.

Children who grow up in an alcohol-influenced environment automatically employ many coping mechanisms in order to deal with the craziness in their household. Unfortunately, these coping mechanisms become so familiar that the children don't learn any other behavior that's not defensive or self-protective. As a result, they end up with a lot of negative baggage they carry into adulthood.

When the child of an alcoholic reaches adulthood without dealing with any of the issues in childhood, that person is then called an adult child of an alcoholic (ACOA). It is in adulthood that the influences of the past really begin to surface, affecting all areas of adult life: relationships, job, marriage, personal growth, and day-to-day decision making.

The ACOA can feel out of sync with the rest of the world. Life can be a daily, sometimes hourly, struggle where he or she may feel like an outsider looking in. The ACOA may desperately want to feel better about life and about him- or herself, but doesn't know where to begin.

There is a "happily ever after" ending in every adult child's fairy tale. That happens when the adult child becomes aware of his or her difficulty in coping with life and seeks help in making some changes.

Individual counseling is a path many have chosen and found great benefits. One of those benefits has been the discovery of nontherapeutic, self-help groups available one or more nights during the week. These groups are called Adult Children of Alcoholics meetings.

Many Adult Children of Alcoholics groups are part of Al-Anon, which was founded shortly after Alcoholics Anonymous for the purpose of helping those whose lives had been affected by someone else's drinking. ACOA is specifically for those who have been brought up in an alcoholic environment. It is open to people who have a history of alcoholism in their family and who have experienced some of the effects of that disease while they were growing up.

The groups have no leaders; rather, they are based upon the principles of the Twelve Steps of Alcoholics Anonymous which teach that each of us is powerless over alcohol and its influences. Through ACOA, members learn how to nurture themselves in a way that helps them foster positive growth for their best benefit.

That's the "happily ever after" for Adult Children of Alcoholics — when they gather up the courage to let go of their past behaviors and concentrate on filling their present and future lives with the positive life skills acquired from self-help programs and therapies.

When an ACOA begins to work on him- or herself, the rewards are just as wonderful as a fairy tale come true.

CASTAWAY

Lynne's Story — Age: 45

Little children should be serene and not scared.

— R. I. *Kimmons*

For years I denied what had gone on in my childhood home, even when I saw my own children exhibiting some of my childhood behaviors. I don't think I really understood the basis for those behaviors until I dealt with the fact that I was a child of an alcoholic parent.

To confront my childhood was difficult because my mind had blanked out many memories. But as the clouds of denial started to clear, I slowly remembered. Then I took a giant step in my recovery and wrote an emotional letter to my deceased mother. In that letter, I expressed my resentments over my childhood and the way she treated me. After I wrote the letter, I reread it and cried in disbelief that my early years had really been like that.

Writing that letter was one of the most cleansing acts I've done since I joined Adult Children of Alcoholics. There have been many others. One of them has been realizing that all of my childhood memories aren't necessarily painful. As time goes on, I trust the loving, warm, gentle memories will come through.

For today, however, I can remember my past without feeling agony and despair. I can look back at my early life and remember it's over and can never be rewritten. All that's important to me now is the present and what I can make of my future.

What once was . . .

I was one of two children in an alcoholic home. My brother was older than I, so we really didn't do much together. My father was an alcoholic. He was a very quiet drunk. In fact, I was never really aware of his drinking problem.

My father never physically abused anyone except one time when he was angry that my mother had taken the car keys when he wanted to go out drinking. He begged and pleaded for them, then finally lost his temper and beat her face. I remember seeing him sitting on the living room couch — triumphant — while my mother looked on with a bruised and battered jaw.

Surprisingly, the issues I have are not with my father. They're with my codependent mother. She mistreated me emotionally and made me feel like a lonely, unneeded castaway.

My mother had some personal problems that contributed to the difficulty we had in our relationship. The first related to her feelings about men. She taught me that men were to be feared, that they could hurt you, and that they could even kill you. Her fears in some ways were real: She had suffered numerous miscarriages and hemorrhages that required hospitalization. Her doctor had even advised her at one point not to sleep in the same bed as my father, or "he'll kill you."

These fears were transferred to me so forcefully that I spent much of my life fearing men. The first time I dated a man, I was filled with anxiety over what might happen when the boy said good night to me. I didn't know what to expect except pain.

My mother's second issue was that my father cheated on her for several years. She eventually discovered he was involved with her best friend. After that, her relationship with me became extremely difficult, as I then became her new best friend and confidante. She made me privy to her personal, intimate feelings. I would be expected to listen to her and help her at a time in my life when I really needed parental guidance and information.

At this time, the mixed messages also started. Even though my mother wanted me to be around to listen to her, she also showed me she didn't really want me around. Despite my father's infidelity, she loved him and wanted the marriage to work. So she made it very clear that my brother and I were interfering with her marriage. We were made to believe that if he and I were out of the house, she and my father could work at fixing their relationship.

I was cast out of the house each summer. My brother and I were shipped off to separate summer camps. He loved his, but I hated mine. Since my family didn't have much money, camp was a doubly painful experience for me because I had to earn my keep there by doing odd jobs like washing the dishes.

I endured the camp for a short time, crying my eyes out every day and making desperate phone calls to my mother. The counselors and camp director tried to keep me from the phone. But I'd fight my way if necessary to make that daily phone call to beg my mother to take me home. One day, I raced to make my call while the rest of the camp was in the dining hall eating lunch. To foil my plans, the counselors had locked the office doors, but that didn't stop me. I climbed through the window and made my call anyway.

I guess I ended up staying at that camp a total of one month. But that one month consisted of 30 days of constant tears and desperate, pleading conversations with my mother when I could get to the telephone. I was miserable. Finally, at the end of the month, my mother came and picked me up. I was so happy to see her that I leaped into her arms. I don't remember her being equally happy to see me. As a matter of fact, she wasn't happy to see me at all. At the end of that summer, I overheard a conversation she had with my brother. She told him I had ruined her entire summer. I remember my brother saying to her, "She's only a kid, Mom. What do you want from her?"

If I could use one word to describe my childhood, it would be *lonely*. I don't really remember having any friends except the ones I invented in my head. I loved to play with my dolls, which I would dress up, talk to, and take for strolls. When I wasn't playing with them, I'd watch a lot of television. In fact, my brother used to tease me and call me a walking T.V. *Guide*. He was absolutely right, because I knew the details of every show.

Outside of home, I had very few friends. I don't think I had the social skills to make friends. I believed only in black and white; you were either right or wrong, rich or poor, on the top or the bottom. There was no middle ground in my mind. So I always tried to be on top, in charge, in control. I wanted to call the shots. I certainly didn't make many friends that way.

I really don't know why I isolated myself so much. I think it was because no one ever seemed to listen to me at home. My father was wrapped up in his drinking, and my mother was wrapped up in the problems between her and my father. No one seemed to notice me or listen to me. I almost died because of this.

One morning I woke up with severe pains on my right side. I told my mother about them, but she thought I was making them up. "You always want to be sick," she said to me. However, she did give in and let me stay home that day, a Thursday.

The next day I had to go to school, even though I told her I still wasn't feeling good. In fact, I was in excruciating pain. I went to school anyway. After school I had to go to the doctor for my weekly allergy shots. I remember walking across a bridge to his office and doubling over in pain every few steps. Then I'd straighten up, walk some more, double over, straighten up, and so on until I got to his office.

I was given some shots and tried not to show anyone the pain I was in. My mother came to pick me up, and I kept silent because I knew she wouldn't believe me.

I remember sitting on my father's lap that night watching television. I turned to him at one point and said, "I hope I feel better tomorrow."

"Of course you will," he replied. "Tomorrow's Saturday."

But that night I couldn't sleep because of the pain, so I lay down on the living room couch and curled up. My mother found me that way and called the doctor. I was rushed to the hospital and into emergency surgery for acute appendicitis.

My parents used to tell me frequently that nice boys and girls don't talk back to their elders. They told me the children who are most loved are the ones who are seen and not heard. My parents were very proud of their quiet daughter, but little did they know I was too scared to say anything. I felt if I said anything I would lose their love. Since I so desperately wanted their love and approval, I remained meek and obedient. I knew if I behaved myself I could earn that love.

I knew my mother loved me, even though I hated the way she treated me, but I never got a sense that my father loved me. I think I struggled for 40 years of my life trying to get his approval. I only received disappointment each time. Perhaps my father was so concerned with pleasing himself and getting what he wanted that he was unable to see his love-starved daughter or the horrible state of his marriage. He did nothing to terminate his relationship with his wife's best friend. He never asked my mother for a divorce, nor did my mother ask him for one. When my mother finally gathered the courage to kick him out of the house — after my brother and I had both left — he went to live with the other woman.

Although I never associated our family problems with my father's drinking, my mother did. She became particularly concerned as his disease progressed. She used to tell me a story about the time she had some friends over to the house and made them vodka gimlets. No one said a word to my mother until she took a sip of her drink and realized it was just a mixer and water — no vodka. My father had drunk all the alcohol and replaced it with water. When my mother confronted him about it, he only laughed and blamed the theft on a young boy who worked in our yard.

As my father's addiction grew worse and his health deteriorated, my mother started to tell me she was going to divorce him. She talked to me about the time when we'd all have to pack our bags and leave the house to go somewhere else to live. This talk made me feel a lot of hope. I felt that if only she'd leave him, everything would be all right. So I would ride the school bus home every day after school and anxiously wonder if "today was the day" that I'd get to pack my bags and leave.

That day never happened. This too she blamed on my brother and me, just as she'd blamed her horrible marriage on us. She and my father had to stay together "for the children. " And that she did. She tolerated his infidelity. She even stayed with him when he was sick with pneumonia and hospitalized. While he was in there I saw him go through the D.T.s, which was horrible to watch. Finally, when I was a senior in high school, my father joined A.A.

My mother then joined Al-Anon. She and I would sometimes go to Al-Anon meetings together or to A.A. meetings with my father. I definitely had program indoctrination at an early age, but I didn't use much of it. I don't really think I believed alcohol was the problem. Although my parents went to A.A. and Al-Anon, nothing seemed to change for the better.

I left home at the age of 21 to live out-of-state with an aunt and uncle. My father's older brother was also an alcoholic, and his family had even more problems than mine. I wasn't there for too long before I dated the man who would become my husband. He too was an alcoholic.

My marriage and my children helped bring many of my adult children issues to a head. My husband's drinking and his behavior helped this happen because he had also been brought up in an alcoholic home. His father had been physically abusive, and my husband used some of those learned behaviors in his relationship with our two sons. Many times our children were hit with a belt or chased through the house.

Then my husband became sick. The diagnosis was a cancerous brain tumor — terminal. Between the alcoholism and the cancer, it was pure madness in my home. I was halfway into and halfway out of denial of the alcoholism in my past and my present. I didn't know what to do. I joined a cancer support group and went into individual therapy. It was there that I was gently eased into looking at myself as an adult child.

What is now . . .

I was encouraged to attend a Claudia Black workshop on Adult Children of Alcoholics but couldn't get in because it was filled. Instead, I was sent a complimentary ticket to see an ACOA film, *Children of Denial*, which I did attend.

I remember reading the handouts at that film, especially the one that lists the fourteen characteristics of an adult child. After reading that and seeing the film, there was no question in my mind that I was in the right place. But what overwhelmed me the most was the number of people at the film. I wasn't alone! I wasn't the only one!

I started going to meetings as often as I could, and I listened and learned. After the first few meetings, it was as if I had a fire underneath me. I was ready to do anything to work through the pain and get over to the side of recovery.

The first thing I had to work on was me. Shortly after I entered the program, my husband died. Suddenly I was a single parent. That was one of the most difficult transitions I ever had to make because I had never before depended upon myself. Even with my alcoholic husband, I was taken care of financially and had all the things I needed. When I was confronted with having to do it all myself, it was frightening and intimidating. I didn't know if I could do it.

But I kept working the program and decided I had to go to work to support myself, and it was going to be a job I liked. I went back to school to get a degree. Even though I was a horrible student when I was growing up, the program gave me courage to see I could change old behaviors and images I had of myself and replace them with something new. The first semester was difficult for me, but I studied hard and ended up doing very well. Since then I've made the Dean's List and received a scholarship based on my academic abilities. I'm not afraid now to earn a degree.

What can be . . .

Today my children are twenty-two, twenty, and sixteen years old. The oldest two are boys. When they were growing up, I couldn't understand why it was so difficult for them and their sister to make friends. I began to see my childhood behaviors in their behaviors, and that realization made me uncomfortable.

One of my greatest hopes is for my children's health and happiness. I see great hope in my daughter because she's making positive changes and has the program to help her. But my sons seem uninterested in program talk and benefits. Although that bothered me at first, I'm learning I have to let them be who they are. I am here to help them when they need it, but they need to come to that decision on their own.

My sons have been a big challenge for me, because of my low self-esteem around males. In fact, once they hit adolescence, the memory of my mother's issues came back to me. I became very intimidated by them and afraid to refuse whatever they wanted.

My daughter and I, however, seem to have a good relationship. She made the decision to attend Alateen after seeing the positive changes in my life. She listens to what the other kids say and applies what she learns to her own life.

I received a magnificent compliment recently from one of my sons. He told me how proud he was of me, my recovery, and how far I've come. It brought tears to my eyes. It's one thing to have a child say he loves you. It's another to hear him say that he's proud of you.

I still don't know what I want to be when I grow up. I think I've made some decisions about school, but I'm trying not to look too far ahead. I do know I want to work in a helping profession, and I feel I'll be very good at that.

Most of all, for right now, I'm trying to learn how to parent myself. I desperately need the parental encouragement and information I never received while I was growing up. Most of the time I feel like I'm trying to relearn how to live. I receive a great deal of positive help and support from the parenting at the ACOA meetings. In fact, it was at an ACOA meeting that I first heard the term, "parenting oneself."

I do that simply by talking to myself and giving myself positive choices. One time I was in a minor car accident and lost the use of my transportation for a while. Rather than becoming angry and upset over the loss, I parented myself through the situation so I had a positive outlook. I told myself I would be all right, there were other people I could call for help, and I didn't have to be devastated by the loss. With parenting, I have become more accepting of life on its own terms.

I do the same kind of parenting in all parts of my life. After having a difficult time with my childhood issues, an ACOA member suggested I write a letter to my mother — even though she was dead — and tell her how I felt growing up at home. One day I got the courage to write that letter, and I've felt wonderful ever since. I spent hours on the letter, detailing my resentment and anger against her.

After I wrote the letter, I reread it. Tears streamed from my eyes, but they weren't only tears of sadness and frustration. They were also tears of cleansing and release. What a wonderful way to get rid of all the negative energy I had carried with me for years! I've reread that letter since that time, but with no tears shed. I have come to terms with my past and am ready to let it go.

Today the letter reminds me where I came from and how far I've come. Every day, I am a little farther down the road to recovery and happiness. Today — and tomorrow — the program helps me cast away the learned behaviors of the past and teaches me the new tools for success. Today I feel I am important, and the parent in me tells me I'm right!

CHILD LABORER

Greg's Story — Age: 37

Courage is being scared to death — and saddling up anyway.

— John Wayne

My biological father was the first alcoholic in my life. I've been told he was physically violent with me, but I don't remember.

Some of my most vivid childhood memories, however, were with my first stepfather. He was probably an alcoholic, but was more noticeably a workaholic. From the age of ten, I spent most of my youth working on his cattle ranch in the western part of the country. Even though that ranch was my home, it sure didn't feel like it. All I did was work, from the moment I got up until the time I went to bed. Sometimes he'd have me go into school late so I could do chores around the ranch. Caring for the cattle took priority over everything else. It wasn't okay to have fun, to share my feelings, or to do things I wanted to. My purpose was to work. I grew up thinking that was all I was good for.

He left when I was fifteen. I left home when I was seventeen and joined the service. Shortly after, I married my first wife out of loneliness. We had our first child, but I didn't know what to do whenever he'd cry. I started to hit him, because that was what my father and stepfather had done with me. Yet deep down I felt that wasn't right.

My alcohol and other drug dependence started. My life was gradually getting out of my control. I began my recovery in A.A., then in ACOA six months later. It was in the adult children's program that I finally came in touch with my fathers' behaviors and how I had never learned what it was like to be a kid.

What once was. . .

There is very little that I remember for the first eight years of my life. During that time, I was living in the West with my mother, father, older sister, and older brother.

I can't remember my father's drinking, nor can I remember his alcoholic behavior. My sister has told me my dad would come home drunk, see all three of us sitting on the couch watching television, and pick me up and start throwing me around the room. Apparently my father physically abused me more than once, but I don't remember.

What I do remember, however, was being punished once by him. It was a "light" spanking with a belt. I recall thinking at the time that the punishment was somehow fair. I realize now why I probably thought it was fair: Compared to the rest of his physical abuse, that time might have been the mildest episode and therefore much easier for me to remember than his more severe punishments.

My father was visibly an alcoholic. There were many times he'd come home from work and be "too tired" for me to wake him. Other times I used to hear my mother say things like, "If your father didn't drink . . . " or "If he'd only recognize that he had a problem . . . "

She divorced my father when I was about eight years old. My sister made her great escape from the family then by getting married. My brother and I were sent to live with my grandparents in another part of the state so my mother could work and pay off some of the bills. We lived with them for almost a year until my mother joined us. Shortly after, she got married again.

My stepfather didn't exhibit a real drinking problem. He'd have a few beers during the week after work, but never got inebriated. At the Saturday night dances he'd usually get visibly drunk. But his drinking problem was minor compared to his workaholism.

My stepfather and I had a slave-to-master relationship. When he and my mother first got married, he purchased a small cattle ranch. My brother and I worked on the ranch by haying and feeding the cattle. It wasn't that bad, because we could handle what work had to be done.

But it wasn't too long before he decided that ranch was too small for him. He wanted to be a big cattle rancher. So he purchased another, much larger ranch with many more head of cattle.

The new ranch was too big for the three of us to work, so the only solution was for him to work my brother and me harder. That ranch became the focus of all our lives. It took priority over everything else.

I remember one of my birthdays shortly after we had started working the bigger ranch. My stepfather gave me a tractor as my gift. At first I was ecstatic, because I looked upon it as a toy and real symbol of manhood to have my own farm vehicle. But, over time, I grew to hate that tractor. The only reason I was given it was to work on the farm. It was a business item to my stepfather, not a gift to his child for his birthday.

There was no time to rest on the ranch. In the summertime, when most kids would be swimming and fishing and taking it easy, I worked hard in the hot, dry fields. In the wintertime, when school was supposed to be the focus, I helped feed the cattle and went to school part-time.

From the moment I awoke, I lived, ate, and breathed the ranch. I couldn't play or have any free time. I had to follow the orders of my stepfather, who would constantly yell at me to get this thing or that thing done. Time became more demanding and more pressured.

At night, when the major work had been done, we'd all gather at the dinner table. Even that time wasn't for relaxing and unwinding. Topics of conversation all had to hinge on the ranch. Most times, there would be plenty of work that needed to be done after dinner. Then, only after all the work had been done for the day, could I finally drop off to sleep.

Growing up, I felt my goal in life was to be a ranch hand. I hated that. There was no time to spend with friends, even though our nearest neighbor lived just a mile away. Most people were miles and miles from us.

I not only felt physically isolated on the ranch, but also emotionally isolated. My parents were too busy to have any time for a family life. There was no time to talk about anything that was going on for me. The only things that were okay to talk about were what I was doing in the fields and how much I'd done.

I remember once I tried to talk to my mother about the fact that my stepfather had been whipping me with a willow. I didn't really know why he had been whipping me, but I didn't feel I deserved the punishment. It hurt so much. So I ran into the house and told her he had been whipping me and why I thought I had been whipped. She later confronted my stepfather with the episode. That set off an explosion in him that made my life even more miserable. The next time he and I were alone he made it very clear to me that I was never to go to my mother again and tell her what was going on.

What was going on was that the man was physically abusing me every chance he could get. I never knew what would precipitate his anger or outrage. Suddenly he'd cuff me. That would usually mean I had done something mild. But if he got out the willow branch, I knew he was really mad at something. It didn't necessarily mean I had done something bad. It just meant he was mad and needed to hit me.

I think he liked to see me cry. I'd usually cry during the willow whippings, because those branches smarted so. But once I figured out that he liked to see and hear me in pain, I got to holding in my tears. I vowed never again would he make me cry. I was twelve years old at the time.

I never did cry in front of him after that, but I had so much physical and emotional pain inside I didn't know how to deal with it. I chose to isolate with my best buddy — my dog. We'd sneak away and go out into the fields, far away from the house, and I'd hold onto that furry neck and cry my eyes out. I wished the whole darn thing would stop — the working, the not talking about feelings, the arguments, and the beatings, and the fact that I couldn't trust anybody. I just wanted it all to get better.

I stayed in that home until I was fifteen. Then my mother divorced my stepfather. Two years later, she married again. My new stepfather was very different from my first stepfather. He didn't have any alcoholic behaviors. He didn't have any workaholic behaviors. I don't think he had any "aholic" in his personality at all. But he did have a behavior that was very difficult for me to deal with: my new stepfather never used physical punishment on me.

With my first stepfather, physical punishments had become a way of life. I grew to believe they were normal. So I didn't know how to deal with the new punishments called "groundings." Sometimes I even went out and did something wrong on purpose, hoping to get a cuff or a whipping. But I got neither. As a result, I mistrusted my mother's new husband and felt very uncomfortable around him.

I left home when I was seventeen. My first destination was college. But I flunked out almost immediately because I didn't go there to learn, but to have a good time. After that, I joined the service.

During the time I was in the service, I lived with my biological father for a few months. That short time was all I needed to come face-to-face with his unpredictable alcoholic behaviors. I soon learned the formula of how to maintain peace with him: sit and listen to him, nodding my head from time to time at all the appropriate spots.

While I was in the service, I dated a woman who was in love with me. She wanted to marry me, but I told her she wasn't the person I wanted to settle down with. But one Thanksgiving vacation I was on the East Coast, far away from my family and feeling very lonely. So I proposed to her. I went into that marriage with a vow to myself that when our first child became eighteen years old, I would divorce my wife.

What is now. . .

I lasted ten years in that marriage. I was pretty heavy into booze and drugs, while she was pretty heavy into depending on me. I was the one who made all the decisions in the marriage. I supposedly had all the power, yet I felt so powerless, especially around my firstborn. If he cried and I couldn't get him to stop, I didn't know what else to do except spank him. I knew that wasn't right, but I really didn't know what I could do that was right.

I stopped spanking him when I started to relate that treatment to the way I'd been treated as a child. Those memories came back to me and I didn't want to feel all that pain. I kept drinking and using drugs and tried to find my happiness.

I moved to the West Coast when I was dissatisfied with my job on the East Coast. Then I met a woman on my business trips amd fell in love with her. I lied to her by telling her I was separated when I really wasn't. I didn't tell my wife a thing, but kept going away on business trips and spending time with my lover.

Finally, after a confusing time of shuttling back and forth from coast to coast, I divorced my wife and married the woman I loved. I thought the new marriage would answer all my prayers and take away all my pain. I struggled to lick my problem with booze by controlling my drinking and trying not to get drunk. A year into my new marriage, I decided alcohol had licked me. I signed up for a treatment center through an employee assistance program.

I first heard the phrase *adult children of alcoholics* at the treatment center. But because I was an alcoholic first, I was told to deal with my addiction. Once I had worked successfully in A.A. for at least six months, then I could investigate the ACOA program.

After six months in A.A., my therapist reminded me of my opportunity to join ACOA. I was ready to jump right in, but that program was more difficult than I thought. In the beginning, I couldn't go to meetings every week. So many feelings would come up for me from my childhood. I couldn't predict what I'd be like after an hour-and-a-half of remembering my childhood and listening to people talk openly about their feelings.

But something wonderful did start to happen at those meetings. As painful as it was to think back to the time I was a little boy, I did start to remember. I forgot all about the vow of a twelve-year-old boy. I started to cry again.

What can be. . .

I've been going to ACOA for almost a year. One of the most difficult and most frightening things for me to deal with in the beginning was the openness and frankness with which people in the program dealt with their feelings. I heard things discussed in those meetings that I never thought were supposed to be discussed. Those topics dealt with feelings.

All my life I believed what I felt wasn't important. I had pretty much been told growing up that I didn't matter. What mattered instead was how much work I could do. But the people in ACOA showed me that I did matter — especially how I felt. They wanted me to share my feelings and wanted to listen to me.

It was difficult to share my feelings because many times that meant I had to look back. I couldn't understand why I needed to look back to my childhood. Wasn't I an adult now? Why did I need to talk about the past? Wasn't it over? Wasn't I supposed to be free from all the feelings of the past? Part of me felt that people were using the past to blame their present-day issues.

But once I started opening up, I discovered I needed to talk about the things that had gone on for me when I was growing up. I began to realize many of my present behaviors were a direct result of past influences. And unless I started talking about them and feeling them, I was never going to let go of their influence over my life.

One area in particular that I got a chance to look at dealt with my feelings about education. I had to take some adult education courses because of my job, but I never really applied myself in those instructional settings. I wouldn't really try hard because it didn't seem to matter. However, after I had been involved in ACOA, I looked back to the education in my childhood and remembered my stepfather had kept me home from school, working as much as possible. Only when I got the work done was I sent off to school. As a result, I was given the message from him that school wasn't important. Therefore, I never learned a whole lot and wasn't very motivated to learn.

Through ACOA, I've not only been able to look back and find some of the answers for my adult behaviors, but I've also been able to use some tools to make changes in those behaviors. I recognize now just how much my emotions drive me. Many of those emotions were molded in the past. I have no control over the past. I can't change that, but I can change today. Now I can work through problems instead of getting frustrated or angry or blaming everything on the whole world.

I'm proud to say today that my anger bouts are farther and farther apart. I haven't thrown furniture for a long time. Staying sober helps me, but letting those old emotions out also works wonders.

Today I'm much more comfortable with myself than I've ever been in my whole life. I'm able to let out my emotions and express them in a positive way.

My home life couldn't be better. We recently had a baby. If I was to have gone through that experience without the help of the ACOA program, I know I would have succumbed to my anxieties and never made it inside the hospital. But I took the courage and strength of the program with me and assisted my wife just the way we were trained.

This new child is beautiful. I know today the right way to communicate with my baby, and that's not through hitting or yelling. With gentleness and open emotional expression, I want my child to be able to experience in every way what childhood is all about.

I'm looking forward to learning how to play with my child.

FIRE AND RAIN

Kitty's Story — Age: 30

Love is not blind — it sees more, not less. But because it sees more, it is willing to see less.

— Julius Gordon

The childhood I remember is filled with wonderful memories. The first ten or eleven years of my life were filled with lots of love and great times of family togetherness.

Then I became aware of my mother's drinking. The warm, loving household I had known changed to a strange place filled with angry emotions and weird behaviors. It was as if I didn't know my mother anymore. This, compounded by my father's serious kidney disease, made life miserable for me. To cope, I gradually began to shut down to the outside world, both emotionally and physically.

If my mother had lived longer, perhaps I could have worked out my feelings toward her. Perhaps she would have sought help in a treatment program or through A.A. These "perhaps" were not to be however. One evening in 1982, my mother was severely burned and rushed to the hospital. Five weeks later, she died.

It took me a long time to get into the ACOA program. In the beginning, it was too painful for me. I wanted to run away. But gradually I started to use the principles of the program. I grew more honest with myself and started to identify areas in my own behaviors that needed work.

Through the fiery pain of my mother's death and the cleansing tears of the program, I have learned to live my life differently — *One Day at a Time*.

What once was . . .

Alcohol was never a problem in my house for the first decade of my life. I recall my parents having daily drinks at six o'clock and together discussing their day. But they never had more than two drinks each, and I never saw them drunk. Even when they drank socially with friends, they never acted differently because of the alcohol.

My parents' devotion was to each other and their children — my older brother and me. We did so many things together as a family. My picture albums are filled with photos of us in the places we traveled to, sights we saw, and activities we enjoyed as a family.

We were always happy and smiling. There never seemed to be any cause for disagreements or anger, other than the usual sibling squabbles. Whenever we had a problem or were upset about something, my parents encouraged us to share our feelings openly.

But that idyllism didn't last forever. When I was eleven or twelve years old, my mom decided to quit the kindergarten teaching job she had held for thirteen years. She had no other job to go to — she just didn't want to do that anymore — so she stayed at home. At first, that was fine and she seemed happy.

A year or so later, however, my dad became very sick. He had always had kidney disease, but now it became worse and he sometimes required hospitalization. Added to that was the fact that his job was gradually losing its security. He worked as treasurer of my mom's family's business — an apple farm — which began to lose money due to difficult growing and harvesting conditions. Because of his illness and the failing business, he had to stop working a full day.

The family's income soon grew smaller. Bills began to pile up. Yard work and home repairs stopped being done. With both my mom and dad at home and little money coming in, the pressures on them began to grow.

Just as my dad was helpless in his disease, so was my mom helpless to change the financial situation. My dad needed her to be there to take care of him. He required dialysis three times a week. Rather than travel into the nearest city hospital, my dad applied for — and received — a grant to be able to dialyze at home on a machine. Although that was convenient, it also placed a burden on my mom because she had to learn how to put my dad safely on the machine. She was trained to fill the role of "head nurse" for those triweekly sessions. I also became involved in those sessions, along with my brother. We were the ones who would be responsible for my dad's care in case anything happened to Mom.

The combination of my father's home care, my mother's joblessness, and the shrinking family income put intense pressure on my mother. She began to focus on alcohol a great deal more. Drinking started to become an obsession for her, rather than a nightly time of sharing with my dad.

Her heaviest drinking nights were the ones when my dad was on the kidney machine. She'd insert the needles in his arm to get him hooked up, then go out to the kitchen, pour herself a drink, and start dinner. She would pour herself many drinks on those evenings.

The effect the alcohol had upon her was quite noticeable. When my mom got drunk, she'd get very vocal and loud. Many times she would throw or break things.

The change in her personality from the wonderful, loving mom I knew was confusing at first, then frightening. Sometimes I'd feel very alone when she was drunk, for I would usually be the only one nearby to see her progressive drinking and the resulting personality changes. My brother, who was two years older than I, was rarely around because he attended private school and was gone for the day until about ten P.M. My dad would be off in a separate room, beginning the six-hour dialyzing process in the afternoon in order to finish by nine or ten o'clock. Then he and my mother would eat dinner together. Although he could hear her loud noises, there was little he could do about it.

I hated being around during those times, because I was put in a position of responsibility. With my dad on the machine requiring attention and my mom behaving like a crazy lady, it was up to me to make sure my dad was safe and protected from her actions. One night, however, things got really out of hand.

On this one particular evening, my mom had been drinking and was becoming very loud. She was frustrated, really frustrated. My dad was in the middle of his dialysis on the machine. She flew into the small room they had set aside for his dialysis equipment and started throwing magazines and books at him, yelling at him at the same time. Each item she threw she tried to aim directly at his arm with the needles in it. She was purposely trying to injure him. I was frightened but didn't know what to do but act helpless.

Fortunately, my brother was home. He grabbed my mom and restrained her from throwing anything else. I raced to my dad to make sure his arm and the needles were all right. He asked me, "Kitty, would you please call the police? She's trying to hurt me." So I did.

Calling the police soon became the only way we could calm Mom down. Before I would call them — when the arguments and destructive behaviors were going on — I would feel shaky and nervous and out of control. But when I dialed the number, a sense of relief would come over me. "Now," I'd think, "things will have to calm down."

Each time the police pulled up to the house and knocked on the door, I'd feel ashamed. My mom's behavior didn't help the situation either, because she would instantly become a different person. It was as if we were the crazy ones. Sometimes she looked at them as if to say, "I have no idea in the world why they called you here, officers. There's nothing happening here out of the ordinary." Throughout my high school years, I frequently called the police.

My mom had always been the calm one in the family. She had been the family's guiding light. She gave us all a sense of direction. But alcohol changed that.

Toward the end of high school, I started to look to my dad for direction. When he was receiving his dialysis, I would feel scared and unprotected. But when he came off the machine, I would feel very safe. He began to do many of the chores around the house that my mom wasn't doing because of her drinking. Although he tried his best, his guiding light didn't shine as brightly as my mom's once had.

When my brother went to college, I moved downstairs to his old room. Lying in bed at night, I would hear the screaming and banging and throwing of things upstairs. I'd lie there alone and wonder whether my parents were going to get a divorce.

But in the morning, activities around the house would proceed as if nothing had happened the night before. My mom would be a wonderful person — all hugs and kisses. For a while, I'd feel satisfied at such a radical change in behaviors. I'd start to think things were really fine and the night before was just my imagination. But such beliefs started to take their toll on me. One way they showed was in the shame I started to feel about my mom's behavior when she drank. She would become loud and nasty, and that was very embarrassing to me.

That shame surfaced in various ways. One night, I sneaked out of the house to meet some friends at the town community center. Somehow my mom found out and drove down to find me. My friends and I ran to the bathroom to hide. We stood up on the toilet seats so my mom couldn't see our feet. We didn't make a sound.

She threw open the door and stormed into the bathroom. She was absolutely roaring drunk. "You're in here, I know you are!" she screamed as she searched for us. She became angry when she couldn't find me, yelled my name four or five times, then gave up and tore out of the building.

That was on a Friday night. On Monday morning, one of my friends grabbed my arm in the school corridor and declared breathlessly, "Kitty, I saw your mom down at the community center. Boy! Was she ever drunk!" I just looked at the girl with no expression on my face and said, "That wasn't my mother."

Each day at home seemed to fray my nerves a little more. The only way I knew how to deal with the hell in my house was to hold everything inside me and try not to feel. If I didn't do that, I knew the feelings I had would overwhelm me so much that I wouldn't be able to concentrate on anything or even do my homework. I started to daydream a lot. My stomach seemed to be in constant turmoil, so I ate very little. I began to lose weight.

After high school, my dad suggested I go away to college. But I didn't like being away from home. As miserable as it had been for me, it was also familiar. I missed my mom and dad. I missed the chaos. I missed the fact that I was needed. So I came home to live with my parents.

My mom's drinking continued to get worse, and her behaviors were starting to be noticed by others. One time, my mom became enraged while some of my dad's family were visiting us. When we tried to restrain her in the kitchen, she bit my dad. In the morning, she had no recollection of her actions. My dad used that incident as a way to convince her that the drinking had to stop.

For three months, she was sober. She was wonderful to get along with, just like the Mom I used to know.

At the end of the ninety days, she asked if she could drink again. My dad said he thought she could handle it, so the drinking resumed. But she couldn't handle her drinking this time any more than she could before. Her behaviors got worse and worse. Sometimes she'd get so drunk she'd get up in the middle of the night and urinate on the rug in the hallway, thinking that was the bathroom. In the morning, she couldn't remember having done that. But the worst was yet to occur.

In May 1982, my mom got really drunk one night. It was very late, and my dad was trying to get to sleep in the bedroom. She was in the kitchen alone, lighting a cigarette. When my dad heard her call his name, he went out to the kitchen. What he saw he couldn't believe.

My mom was standing in front of him; what remained of her nightgown was smoldering around her wrists and her neck. The rest of the nightgown had caught fire and burned to her. My dad ran to her, put out the lingering fire near her wrists, then called the ambulance.

She was rushed from the local hospital to a city hospital with third degree burns on more than 60 percent of her body. She had a 50/50 chance of pulling through. I refused to believe she was going to die, even when the doctors were quite clear about the severity of her condition. I remember my denial as I snubbed the doctors and said, "You don't know my mother. She'll live through this. " I believed her accident was the lesson she needed to learn to get sober. When she got well, I thought, she would then deal with her alcoholism and things would be fine.

But I never got the chance to see that happen. After five weeks in intensive care, she died.

What is now . . .

Three weeks after my mom died, I had my first one-on-one therapy appointment with a psychologist. Its purpose was for me to deal with the feelings I had because of my mom's death, her alcoholism, and the behavior patterns I had unknowingly developed to cope with my mom's disease.

The psychologist helped me realize that not only was my mom an alcoholic, but she had also died a typical alcoholic's death. When she said that, I remembered the hospital personnel had told me how common it was for drinkers to be admitted with burns. At the time, I didn't pay much attention to that statement, but now I had to. I also had to pay attention to just how severe my mom's illness was. I had to accept the fact that she was an out-of-control alcoholic. I had to accept reality: her disease had been incurable and the only way she could've gotten better was to stop drinking and work on herself in the A.A. program. I was told I couldn't deny the severity of her disease nor the finality of her death any longer.

After three months of individual therapy, I enrolled in an Adult Children of Alcoholics therapy group. There I learned that my own inappropriate behaviors and coping mechanisms weren't so unique. I was encouraged to attend regular ACOA meetings, but I refused for a long time.

Finally, in 1984, I went to my first ACOA meeting. During the meeting, I nearly got sick to my stomach. I could hardly wait for the meeting to be over. When it was, I raced home and stayed under the covers for the rest of the day. What scared me in the meeting was the openness and honesty everyone had about their feelings. They talked about their fears, loneliness, pain, and shame in a very relaxed, accepting manner. How could they do that, I wondered. Those were all the feelings I had suppressed for years so I didn't have to feel them. If I didn't want to feel them, how could I even start to talk about them?

But despite these initial fears, I kept going to the meetings. For the first few months, I didn't say a word to anybody. I didn't talk during the meeting, to anyone at break, or even after the meeting. I'd just run home and suppress the feelings that had been stirred up.

What I took home with me, however, gradually started to sink in. I began to recall the wisdom and strength in what many of the people had shared. I heard people say how good it felt for them to open up. I heard them express relief in being able to talk about what it felt like to grow up in an alcoholic home.

Through those people, I began to learn a lot about myself. As I listened to others, I found I could identify with many of their feelings. I heard people talk about trust and knew I really didn't trust anybody. I found out I wasn't the only one who was afraid of people.

Slowly, I began to open my mind to the tools of the ACOA program. After a year, I volunteered to make coffee for the group and unlock the door to the meeting. I started to stay after the regular meeting for the monthly business meeting. I started to talk with others and ask for telephone numbers. ACOA meetings became a part of my weekly schedule of things I needed to do for me.

What can be . . .

I do not want to die an early death because of this disease. Before I entered the ACOA Program, I was already involved with A.A., Al-Anon, and Narcotics Anonymous (N.A.) because I had increased my use of alcohol and other drugs after my mom's death in order to cope with the pain. But deep down inside I was petrified I would end up dying like my mom did. Each of the programs gave me insight into myself.

In ACOA meetings I discovered that all the shields I had used to protect myself while coping with my mom's disease needed to be put aside in favor of healthier methods of coping.

I once believed that suppressing feelings meant they wouldn't be felt. I used to deal with reality by not dealing with reality. But today I know I can live a long and fulfilling life if I use the tools of the program. These tools tell me I need to share my feelings and meet reality with both eyes open.

I'm learning today how to be honest with myself and with other people. I recently started work on my Fourth Step inventory and confronted many of my shortcomings and character defects. I've asked someone to be my sponsor and am working with her by talking about things happening in my life.

But perhaps the greatest gift I've been given from the program is the ability to stay in the present. I used to worry about the past and dread the future. Many times I even used to put my feelings off, saying, "Well, I'll feel sadness tomorrow when I have a few hours to myself."

Today I can feel sad at the moment I feel sad. I work on all my current feelings and issues in the present. As a result, life is a great deal simpler because it's not cluttered or complicated with thoughts of the past or the future. I just think about now and today.

There's a great deal more work for me to do, however. The program has helped me identify those areas. Just by doing that, I know I've fought half the battle. For the rest, I know I can let go and let my Higher Power work with me to achieve the goals I have set for myself.

One goal is to develop my self-esteem. Another is to continue to learn more about my sexuality and deal with issues of intimacy. I also want to feel closer to my friends. I want to learn how to trust them. These things I know I can do, as long as I work the program.

If my mom were alive today, I would want her to be sober and in the program. I would want her to be living a way of life that I now enjoy and I know other alcoholics enjoy. I feel she was cheated out of her life because of alcohol.

I know her death at such a young age was a real tragedy. But, as I understand the definition of a tragedy, it's something you bring on yourself. My mom definitely caused that accident. Nobody else is responsible for her behavior while she was alive or the circumstances of her death.

I loved my mom, and told her that many times during her life. I am grateful for the wonderful memories I have of her and for the love I still feel for her. Although she is gone, she is still a part of me in many ways. Despite the tears and the anger I experienced because of her, I am where I am today because of her. Today, I am healthy, happy, and sober — and living One Day at a Time.

IN IT FOR THE FUN

Stan and Danielle's Story — Ages: 36 and 31

Some parents bring up their children on thunder and lightning, but thunder and lightning never yet made anything grow.

— Anonymous

We've been married since 1982, but can honestly say that the largest growing we did as a couple was after 1984. For, in that year, we both joined Adult Children of Alcoholics.

Up until that time, our marriage had raised a number of uncomfortable issues for each of us. We were both afraid of intimacy and honesty. We were both hesitant to trust and be vulnerable. We both suffered from a low sense of self-esteem.

While our marriage was far from being doomed, these issues were beyond our individual abilities to solve. But Adult Children's meetings gave us the key to unlock the door to make many things in our marriage better — from our own individual health to the ability to have quality communication with each other.

It was in Adult Children's meetings that we came face-to-face with the past. We were confronted with the memories of what it was like for both of us to grow up in alcoholic homes. Once we dealt with those emotions individually, we were ready to share them with each other. Gradually, many of the secrets of our youth were revealed.

For the past two years in the program, our communication has improved 100 percent. That's helped us to get closer to each other. As a result, we're discovering a great deal about each other — who we are, why we act the way we do, and what goals we've set for ourselves.

Our marriage, like us, is on the road to recovery.

What once was . . . for Danielle . . .

I was the older of two daughters. My parents instilled in me an overdeveloped sense of responsibility, mostly to benefit others rather than myself. As a result, I had to be the example for my younger sister. I took my superachiever role quite seriously, making sure I always got good grades and was friendly and easygoing with everyone.

My father was the alcoholic. While I never saw him drink openly around the house, I knew there was alcohol available. At first I liked my father and didn't have very many problems getting along with him. When I turned thirteen years old all that changed, for that's when my father's disease affected him in a way that was very frightening. That's when my father started sexually abusing me.

I began to date in my early teens, but my father was very overprotective of me. The incest then started, with him coming into my bedroom at night and kissing me in a way that was not a normal father-daughter kiss. He also began touching me in places I knew he shouldn't.

I felt very strange and uncomfortable with what my father was doing. Many times I wanted to tell someone about him, like my sister, but he scared me into not telling anyone. Like the good, dutiful daughter I was, I didn't tell for a long, long time. In fact, the incest continued for two years.

Then one night all hell broke loose and the truth became known. I had skipped school one day, but my sister had lied to cover for me. She got caught in her lie and my father started punching her as punishment. Seeing him hurt her sent me into a rage. After enduring all those nights with my father — holding onto my sick, sick secret — I knew I wanted to kill him for what he had done. He wasn't going to hurt anyone else anymore — not me and not my sister.

I started hitting him as hard as I could, with every intention of hurting him as much as I could. My mother raced into the room when she heard all the fighting to find out what was going on. I desperately screamed out to her that I had something to tell her, something that she never knew about my father and me.

My father whirled toward me, his face full of rage, and yelled, "Shut up!" But I didn't shut up. I blurted out the whole story to my mother. I told her he was doing things to me physically that weren't right, that he was touching me in places that he shouldn't have been touching me. I was crying and shaking at the same time.

The only thing my mother did was stand there in silence.

In that silence, my father hit me hard on the head and left the room. I looked at my mother, hoping for some sign of caring or compassion. She didn't reach out to me. She didn't say a word.

I raced to my room and stayed there for hours until I went to the kitchen for a drink of water. My mother met me there and asked if I was all right. I couldn't believe she was asking me such a ridiculous question! Of course I was all right. But things were all wrong, and I wanted them to be fixed and receive some understanding and love and compassion for what I had gone through. I got nothing from her.

That night I lay in bed, hoping I'd hear them talking about what I had revealed. I never heard a word.

I was a senior in high school, and all I could think of was how to get out of that unbearable situation. I left home after graduation and moved a few states away. I took a job as a waitress in a small restaurant. Two years later, my parents divorced and my father tracked me down to the small town where I was living.

When he walked unannounced through the restaurant doors that day, all the old fears I had about him came back. I started crying hysterically. He asked me where I was living. I was so afraid to tell him, for fear he'd come there and abuse me again. When he left that day, I prayed to God he wouldn't come near me. My prayers were answered. After that, I never saw him again.

During the two years I had been away from home, I hadn't had any contact with my mother. It seemed she didn't want anything to do with me, as if she were ashamed of what I had done with my father. But when she remarried, she and my stepfather came into my life. That made me feel good and gave me a small sense of belonging. When I made the decision to quit the waitressing job and move somewhere else, I was told I was welcome to live with them.

The first month back at home was fine, but the second and third were pure hell. I wouldn't go into the house unless my mother was there too, because I was afraid if my stepfather and I were there alone she would think he and I had been doing something. I felt very tense in the house and decided I had to get out on my own.

I moved out when I was 25 years old. Before I left, my mother told me she loved me — the only time she ever had said that. I left the house knowing that I had to start feeling better about myself, no matter what she or anyone else felt about me.

Soon I had my own apartment, a nice job, and good friends. For entertainment, I went out to a bar for some drinking and dancing. That's when my life really changed, for I met Stan — Mr. Wonderful.

What once was . . . for Stan . . .

I am the middle son of three boys. My older brother was the one who had to set the benchmarks for my younger brother and me. I had to either meet these standards or better them. If I didn't, I was made to feel like a failure.

My father was the alcoholic, but he had stopped drinking two years before he married my mother. It wasn't his choice to stop, but a response to my mother's ultimatum of, "It's either me or the bottle." He chose her and went on a long dry drunk.

The "ism" of the alcoholism affected my relationship with my father in many ways. First, I learned to accept the fact that my father would never tell me he loved me or show me any open affection. I never expected him to be anything but the hard man that he was, very set in his ways, as unmoving as a rock.

Second, I learned to accept the fact that my father was very much the authority figure in the house. What he said was to be listened to and obeyed.

Third, I learned to fear my father. Growing up, I knew I had to toe the line. If I didn't, I would be severely beaten with a strap on my naked buttocks. I remember exactly how it used to be: do something wrong, get caught, go into the bathroom, drop the pants, bend over the bathtub, get beaten severely on the butt.

One of the things I knew I'd get beaten for was not coming home as fast as my father wanted me to when he called me. He'd venture out on the front steps of the porch and call me at the top of his lungs. He had a voice that projected over fields, mountains, and streams. When I heard it, I'd run home as fast as I could. By the time he called out a second time, I was sure to be almost home no matter how far away I'd been. If I wasn't, I was sure to be beaten.

I was a lonely, fat child with very few friends. In fact, the only friends I really had were in my imagination. In my head, I was the popular guy, the hero, the crowd pleaser, the leader of the gang. My fantasies always involved "Stan and the Guys." We were always out to do really heroic things, like save the fort or the wagon train, or beat the hell out of the Sheriff of Nottingham.

Because of my weight, I had to go through the abuse of hearing I was "Fat Stan" from many kids. That's why I was lonely; I learned to isolate from them and stay away from their abuse. But other people had their own nicknames for me. My father's favorite nickname for me was "louse." I thought it was a term of affection until I learned what it meant.

When I got older, I tried to find acceptance elsewhere. This led me to the world of drinking, using drugs, and life in the fast lane. I loved it because it gave me a sense of belonging. After work on the late shift, a bunch of the guys and I would go down to the local bar, party, and close the place down.

It was there that I met Danielle.

Because of the alcohol the night that we met, we were intimate right from the start. But as time went on, we began to see each other as two people in a committed relationship.

We were both, however, afraid of this commitment. Because of our backgrounds, we didn't want to share an awful lot or become close. There was an unspoken fear of our really getting to know who the other person was. We both felt we didn't deserve the relationship, even though we both ached to be loved.

We were drawn together for the fun of it. We loved excitement. We liked fast lane things. Things went fairly well for a while, until something happened to make us break up.

Danielle . . .

When I found out I was pregnant, I wanted to break up with Stan. He wanted to get married. But neither one of us really was very mature about the whole thing. We should have taken precautions right from the very beginning, but neither one of us wanted to take any responsibility. We were just having a good time.

After talking about it, I made the decision to have an abortion. Stan paid for it, drove me there, and tried to take care of me. He was kind and loving to me all day, but I just kept pushing him away. I cried the whole day. I was crying for shame, for the loss of the child, for guilt, and for feeling cheap and dirty. That day, I felt like I had when my father abused me.

I decided to leave Stan and go out with another person I had dated before I met him. For many weeks, I was torn between my affection for this other man and my love for Stan. I eventually came back to Stan because I saw such a kind, loving person in him. I knew he was someone I really wanted to be with. When we got back together, we decided to try living together.

Stan . . .

When Danielle told me she was pregnant, I discovered I was in the really familiar role of victim. In all my other relationships with women, I always let them dominate and control me and never stood up for me. With Danielle's pregnancy, she was in the position of control and I was the victim. But I did want to marry her, not only out of a sense of responsibility and guilt, but also because I really did love her and felt the love she had for me. I knew I didn't want to lose her.

It really hurt when she wanted to go back with the other man, because Danielle had been the one who really held us together. She was the one who really believed in the relationship, right from the start. She seemed so sure that she really wanted me and didn't want to let go.

Her commitment to the relationship was something I had never felt before. I noticed I had begun to change — for the better. I was starting to take more responsibility for myself and my actions.

It was difficult to let her go, but I knew she needed to have some freedom and time to think things over. I knew if she came back, things would be fine. When she finally did come back, I was on cloud nine.

When we started living together, I found myself once more in the role of victim. Danielle was like a figure towering above me, hanging over me and scolding, "Bad boy, Stanley. You didn't put water in the milk glass and now there's going to be a ring in it to scrub out. " Danielle was definitely the domineering one, the authority figure. Glasses had to be scrubbed, towels had to be hung just right. She demanded perfection of me right down the line. And I ate it right up because I felt like I had never left home. It was very comfortable for me.

Despite Danielle's controlling behaviors, I knew she was the woman I wanted to spend the rest of my life with. There was so much love coming from her. She showed me she needed me. And I knew I needed her.

Danielle . . .

Living together was fun, but I became the superresponsible Danielle I had been when I was growing up. I felt I had to set the standards for Stan, tell him what to do and how to do them. I left very little room for compromise. Things had to be done my way or no other way. There were no mutual agreements for me.

We really did love each other. He told me I was the one he wanted to spend the rest of his life with. I felt the same way with him. I wanted to be his responsible, loving wife.

Both of us had dreams we shared. We wanted the house with the white picket fence. We wanted the two-car garage and the comfortable life. We wanted to travel, to have a family.

But, most of all, I wanted somebody there to love me. That's all I wanted. That's all I ever wanted.

What is now . . . for Danielle . . .

We were married in September 1982. But Stan's addiction to alcohol and other drugs took their toll on the marriage, and he went away to treatment in 1984. During his last week of treatment, I went to the same place for the family program.

Besides dealing with Stan's addiction, I found out I also had to deal with what it was like for me to grow up in an alcoholic home. The counselors there recommended I attend Adult Children of Alcoholics meetings when I got back home, which I did.

At first it was scary. I was so afraid that everything from my past — all my secrets — would come out. Up until that point I hadn't really shared with anyone the details of the relationship with my father, and I didn't know how I'd handle them once I started talking about them. It took me a while to open up, but I couldn't have chosen a safer place. The meetings felt very spiritual. The people there were taking risks and sharing their feelings. Soon I was opening up too and doing quite a bit of crying in the process.

After a few meetings, I asked Stan to go with me for support.

What is now . . . for Stan . . .

When Danielle asked me to go to her ACOA meetings, I thought it was only fair since she was supporting with my meetings. But the first one I went to, I was blown away. I remember to this day who spoke and what he said. And, while I didn't identify with the circumstances of that speaker's childhood, I could more than identify with his feelings. They were my feelings too.

The first few times we went together, we sat next to each other. But Danielle started trying to take care of my feelings rather than focus on her own. So I sat apart from her in the room.

After a while, we started talking to each other in intimate details after the meeting. It was then that I really found out about all the things that had happened in Danielle's past, including the incest.

35

Danielle . . .

I was scared for Stan to know what had really happened to me. It had been very difficult for me to shake the blame about the incest, and I was afraid if I told Stan he would blame me too as a guilty party.

But Stan was kind and understanding. He shared equally with me about his childhood, talking about the loneliness he had felt and the kind of person his father had been to him.

The sharing that began after that meeting brought us a lot closer. We attended an ACOA meeting on Sunday morning. After that meeting, and usually long into the afternoon, we would have some of the greatest talks we'd ever had. They were meaningful, intimate conversations — some of the first we'd ever had in our marriage. I found out so much about Stan, and he learned so much more about me.

Stan . . .

The ACOA meetings kicked the lock right off the door that guarded secrets from our past. I found out about the incest in Danielle's past and she found out about the lonely, chubby little boy and how he felt when he was growing up.

Our sharing gave me more of an understanding about my wife. I got to see why she thought the way she did and acted the way she did. I got to know her on a more personal level than I ever had.

For her to know me was scary at first. I had kept walls up for so long, even for the years we had lived together and first been married. I didn't want to be vulnerable with her. I'm more comfortable being vulnerable with her now than I used to be, and that's helped me learn about trust. I have a great deal more trust in Danielle than I ever had at any time in our marriage.

What can be . . . for Danielle . . .

I basically found myself in the program, and I'm really happy I did! I want to keep the self-esteem I've earned and the confidence I've gained. More than anything, I want to go after the challenges that lie before me — in making myself a better person as well as helping to make my relationship better.

In my marriage, I want the sharing and honesty to continue to grow. I want to have a willingness to listen to Stan and to remain nonjudgmental of him, no matter what he needs to say.

I want us to keep growing. ACOA has given us a whole new way of life and a renewed hope for a long-term marriage.

What can be . . . for Stan . . .
I want to continue to use ACOA to help me find the emotional balance in my life. I don't want to be ecstatically happy or incredibly miserable. I want to be somewhere in the middle of the road, with no blacks or whites, rights or wrongs, good or bad.

In my marriage, I want to be an honest husband in the things I say. I need to continue to open up and share with Danielle so she can continue to know me. If I don't, I'm not only cheating myself but also the marriage.

There's a lot of turmoil that goes into a relationship where there are two untreated adult children. This turmoil can be inwardly felt or outwardly exhibited. But we made the decision to save our relationship from the ghosts of the past that haunt Adult Children of Alcoholics.

We owe it to ourselves to continue to go to ACOA so our relationship is constantly given the tools it needs to keep growing. Our marriage can't stay the same all the time because there's always room for improvement.

For us, our marriage is dead and gone if we believe it can't grow anymore. Today our marriage is growing like a newly planted garden. With the sunshine and nourishment of the program, we will continue to grow healthy and strong — both as two individuals and as a couple.

TOO MUCH ALIKE

Mary Ellen's Story — Age: 36

A child is a person who can't understand why someone would give away a perfectly good kitten.

— Doug Larson

Looking back, I remember an incredible sense of loneliness that was eased for many years by my relationship with my grandfather. I loved him. He was my best friend and my hero. Then something happened that destroyed our wonderful relationship. That incident was to influence me for years.

My grandfather was the first alcoholic in my life. The second was my mother. The third was my husband. But the fourth alcoholic in my life meant the most to me. That alcoholic was me.

During my own recovery, I had to confront the fact that not only was I an alcoholic, but I was also the child of an alcoholic. Not only did I have to become sober, but I also had to take a painful look at my childhood. I had to remember the feelings I had about my relationships with my alcoholic grandfather and my alcoholic mother.

The program taught me, in a gentle way, that I finally had to put to rest the intensely negative feelings I had toward my grandfather. That was hard for me, because my feelings towards him weren't always so negative. In the beginning, we had a marvelous friendship built upon closeness, trust, and kinship. I got along with him better than anyone, for he and I were very much alike.

What once was . . .

I lived with my mother, father, and older brother in an apartment building just outside the city. My grandparents lived downstairs from us, and I visited them frequently.

In my preschool years, I was a lonely kid. I never wandered very far from home or crossed the street to see what was on the other side. I don't think I even had the desire to stray from my home or backyard. I think I felt a little afraid of being too far from my home or my family.

39

This feeling continued even when I started going to school. I remember an incident in kindergarten. I was standing outside of the school on an early release day. For some reason, my mother didn't know I had to be picked up early. I stood and watched as, one by one, all the other kids left. Then, I was alone. A feeling of panic crept over me as I imagined my mother would never come and get me and I would never be able to go home and feel safe and secure with her and my grandfather. Finally, a teacher drove me home.

Once I was home, it didn't matter that I was a lonely, isolated child. As far as I was concerned, I had everything I ever wanted in my house, for in my house lived the very best friend anyone could want — my grandfather.

I spent a lot of time on my grandfather's lap. When he'd come home from work I'd run down to see him and we'd watch television together. We'd laugh at *Pinky Lee* and *Howdy Doody* like we were best friends. He seemed to look forward to our TV times as much as I did. In a way, he had this child inside of him, and I think that's what made us think and feel and act so much alike.

Like any child, I remember really wanting to have a pet around the house. Then, one night, my grandfather surprised me with a kitten. Except this wasn't any ordinary kitten — this was a wild alley cat kitten! I loved it and was so excited! But my mother and grandmother didn't share my enthusiasm. They said I had to leave it downstairs with my grandparents so it could stay warm next to their stove. I think I knew something was fishy at the time, but I obeyed them without much protest. But the next morning, the kitten was gone. They told me it had disappeared during the night.

I was heartbroken. I knew my grandfather hadn't taken the kitten away from me, I knew it was the doing of my mother and grandmother. At the time, I felt there were two sides to the family. My mother and grandmother were on one side; my grandfather and I were on the other. My own father didn't seem to be on any side, although he was jealous of the relationship I had with my grandfather. But I didn't care. I loved my grandfather.

I think my grandfather would have been my best friend throughout all my school years if it hadn't been for his drinking. Although I believe he drank for many years, I don't seem to recall alcohol being a problem in the beginning of my relationship with him. But after a while, I began to notice the change in his behavior when he was drunk. It was a complete character change, like a Jekyll and Hyde transformation. One minute he'd be my sweet, loving grandfather, and the next minute he'd seem like Satan himself.

He was a very angry man when he was drunk. Although I was never the brunt of his temper, I could hear my grandmother taking it all. I remember questioning in my mind why she would let herself be screamed at so loudly. My grandfather would stay up late, screaming obscenities at her. Once in a while, my mother would attempt to calm him down, but she didn't seem to be very effective.

Whenever my grandfather's drunken rampages happened, the house seemed totally out of control. Yet no one seemed capable of making things better. My father was wrapped up in his career, so he didn't seem to want to get involved. My brother, who was five years older than I, had no problem with isolation or loneliness, so he was off doing older-brother things. I listened to the raging of my grandfather and saw no one doing anything to stop him. I thought that either my family was insane or I was. When no one else seemed to notice the crazy behaviors, I began to think I was the one who was insane.

Then my grandmother fell and broke her hip. For some reason, this woman who was supposed to be in the hospital under close medical care was taken back to her apartment to recover. My mother became more active in two ways at this time. First, she became very protective of my grandmother, choosing at times to stand up to my grandfather as she slaved to take care of my bedridden grandmother. Second, her drinking increased. She was starting to be on a thin edge herself, not only caring for her family but also caring for an infirm elderly person and trying to keep my grandfather's behavior in line.

One night something happened that was to alter the relationships in our family dramatically. It was a typical night: my grandmother lay incapacitated in her bed while my drunken grandfather screamed obscenities at her. I had been asleep, but was awakened by the shouting. I heard my mother rush from her bedroom and go down to their apartment, presumably to stop the fighting. I was aware of some of this in a half-asleep state.

Then I heard someone being hit. I heard someone fall to the floor. I jumped out of bed and ran to the top of the stairs, not quite knowing what to do. I saw my mother stagger up the stairs, crying about her blackened eye. She ran right into my arms for comfort, just like a little girl. I held her as if I were her mother and decided to take action against my grandfather.

41

I raced down to my grandparents' apartment. My grandfather was completely naked, racing around my grandmother's bed while screaming at her. I felt a rage inside me as I screamed at him, "If you ever do that again, I'll kill you! You get into bed now, or I'll never speak to you again!" Surprisingly, he did. For the rest of the night, the house was quiet. But that night was the end of my close relationship with my grandfather.

The next day, he offered me some money to buy a treat. I took the money, but that didn't change the way I felt toward him. I vowed to never forgive him.

Shortly after that, my grandmother died. I remember coming home from school and seeing strange people sitting in our kitchen and talking. Someone said, "Mary Ellen, your grandmother's dead." I went to a window, looked out over the city, and said to myself, "These people are never going to see me show my feelings — ever!" I made a decision not to cry that day and never to let anyone into my life like I had my grandfather. My grandfather remarried not long after my grandmother's death. Fortunately, he moved out of the apartment. I was glad to see him go.

I spent some time in school struggling to make friends, even though people seemed to like who I was. I was elected to class offices and invited to do things with people. But it wasn't until I got to high school that I felt really comfortable being close friends with people. Then I met some people I really cared about. I wasn't alone anymore. I even had a best friend.

With my grandfather's drinking behavior out of our lives, I felt our family would soon become sane. But one alcoholic was replaced with another. My mother went into a real depression and started drinking heavily and often. One night was particularly embarrassing for me. We all went out to a restaurant for dinner — my mother, my father, my brother, and I. My mother wanted me to come to the bathroom with her, so we walked there together. But on the way, my mother staggered, then stumbled and crashed headlong into a radiator. She was briefly knocked unconscious, and a curious circle of onlookers formed before my father was summoned. While I was standing over her, not certain what to do, she regained consciousness, looked at me, and asked, "Who are you?"

My mother's drinking got worse and worse. She was so jealous of my friends and especially jealous of my best friend. After that incident with my grandfather, all she seemed to want to do was cling to me. It was almost a complete role reversal of mother and child. She now expected me to take care of her, which I didn't want to do. She would almost devour me at the end of my school day, springing upon me the minute I came into the house. She'd hammer me with questions: "How was your day?" "What did you do?" By that time, she would already be drinking. I would plead with her to go out and get a job, to do anything but sit around the house all day, depressed and drinking. But she'd get angry at such suggestions.

I think deep down inside she was probably screaming for love and attention, but I felt smothered by her and didn't want to give it. I had had enough of the alcoholic behaviors with my grandfather, and I was disgusted by her immaturity. Her behavior was very similar to the mother in *Long Day's Journey Into Night*. At eight P.M., she'd announce she was going to bed. By that time her speech would be incoherent and she'd be staggering. I'd be glued to the television, praying for her just to shut up and leave the room. She'd wander off to her room, but soon come back just to pat me on the head and say how much she loved me.

Many times I'd feel guilty and sad for her. I didn't know at the time all the clinical jargon to describe what she was going through, but I did know she was feeling a great deal of unhappiness and pain. Sometimes when my guilt would overwhelm me, I would open the door to my feelings a crack and tell her something in confidence. But usually she'd respond with "Oh, dear, you shouldn't feel that way," or she'd take on some of the feelings and start to worry and obsess about them. The burden of handling my own feelings and then hers was too much for me, so I soon learned not to share anything with her.

As I became more apathetic toward her, I slowly accepted her drinking. I wasn't aware of alcohol as a real problem. I was aware that people drank, but I really didn't believe alcohol was the actual culprit. When I was younger I viewed the liquor store as a truly magical place that we stopped at frequently to buy beer for my parents. And, once in a while, I'd get to share in some of that magic when I'd be given a juice glass of beer while I watched television.

So when my mother began to offer me drinks when I was in high school, she didn't have to twist my arm to get me to accept. The fact was, I really enjoyed drinking. I also had the feeling, "If you can't beat 'em, join 'em." In my teenage years I started to drink heavily. Much of my drinking was done in my own home with my mother.

I continued drinking heavily when I began to date men. I honestly didn't even want to go through the dating process. If I had had a choice, I would've partied with my girlfriends as much as I could. But I really didn't believe I had a choice. I had been raised to believe my purpose in life was to get married and raise a family. I had also been shown that men were the focal point of a marriage. I learned from my mother that my father's career and interests came first, even though that meant she had to sit around the house feeling lonely and depressed. I learned from my grandmother that all my grandfather's behaviors were to be tolerated and excused.

It was with this background that I went into a six-year relationship with a man I was later to marry. This relationship was quite tolerable. He was in the military and therefore hardly ever around. When he did come home on leave, I merely dropped what I was doing, and paid attention to him for his stay. I spent the rest of the time partying with my friends.

We were married as soon as he got out of the service. A year later, I had my first child. I remember setting a mental goal that I would stop drinking when the child was born, because my drinking had escalated to a point where I was worried. I was beginning to recognize I had a drinking problem, but I didn't believe I was alcoholic or that my drinking was out of control. I just remembered my childhood and vowed to never be a drunken mother or raise my children in the kind of home I had been raised in.

My marriage situation didn't help. In the space of five years we moved five times. In the last move, I found myself in a suburb far from friends or potential friends. I spent a great deal of time drinking with my husband, who also had a drinking problem. His drinking was beginning to affect me negatively. Sometimes I'd see him drunk and, in a flashback, see my grandfather. One night my husband was really irritating me, and I punched him in the arm so hard that the next morning he could hardly move it. This anger reminded me of my grandfather's anger, and I realized I hadn't ever forgotten him or the pain he had caused me.

I was really scared at the way my behaviors were surfacing. What was happening to me? I pleaded with him for us to go to marital counseling. He agreed. I had even become worried about my own drinking and asked the marriage counselor if I might be an alcoholic. He asked me one or two questions about my drinking patterns, and then assured me I was not an alcoholic.

So, once again, I held onto the teenage attitude I had had toward my mother's drinking — if you can't beat 'em, join 'em. I continued drinking heavily with my husband for the next two years.

What is now . . .

On May 28, 1979, I was at my grandfather's house, helping him paint. Seven months before, I had been in individual counseling trying to stop drinking. My husband had stopped attending marital counseling because he believed I was the one with the problem. But after three days around my grandfather, I began to wonder about my behavior around alcoholics. My grandfather's behavior hadn't changed at all, but once again, I became just like my grandfather. I went out and bought a six-pack.

I drank that six-pack and realized I was going nowhere with just counseling. I remembered my new counselor had told me, "Therapy is good for a year or two, but A.A. is for life. " I finally had to admit I was beat and couldn't do it on my own. I joined A.A.

I was in A.A. for a couple of years. Sobriety was incredible for me, because it helped me open my eyes to all that was happening around me. I realized I was behaving as a typical adult child. I believed I had no options, no control over my life, and no power in my relationships or my life. I saw that my husband had a decent office job, yet we lived like paupers. He never allowed me to make a decision. I always had to abide by his. He was both in control and out of control because of his drinking. I went to my meetings and came back each night to a home life that I was beginning to see more and more clearly. I began to see many similarities between the way I was living and the way my mother and grandmother had lived.

As long as I stayed in my marriage with a drinking spouse, I was reminded of my alcoholic background. I was brought up in fear, frustration, and anger and began to live my adult life with the same components. The more I was sober, however, the less I wanted to live in it.

In my third year of sobriety, I had had it with my husband and filed for divorce. It was the worst mess of my entire life because he countersued for the children. In his suit, he claimed that since I was attending A.A. meetings, I was a known alcoholic.

In the midst of the mess, I went home to my parents. It was a great day for me, because I could see how far the program had brought me. I let my parents be there and give me help. They were extremely supportive. This time, I wasn't afraid to be open and let my parents see my personal feelings. I was ready to take more risks.

Through the sobriety, I was able to see the reality of situations. I remember before I got myself into A.A. — just about the time I reached my bottom — I was sitting in the living room with my children. I could see them and hear them, but it was as if I was sealed in a plastic bubble. I felt distant and removed from them and somehow not quite right.

Sobriety took the bubble away. I could see my children clearly and give my love to them freely. Even if my marriage couldn't work out, I knew that was okay. Even when my husband countersued and we ended up with shared custody, I knew that was okay too. I became more accepting.

What can be . . .

It wasn't too long before I realized I had reached a certain limit in my growth in A.A. I couldn't depend upon the A.A. program solely to give me all the tools I needed to handle situations in my life. Once I met another person and we began living together, I started doing the same stupid things I did in my marriage. Even with two recovering alcoholics in one household, neither of us was prepared for the issues that came up.

I had the same old sense of powerlessness and fear and frustration in this new relationship. I began feeling everything I did was wrong or my fault. I started to feel that I needed approval for everything I did. If I didn't get it, I felt I was wrong. That's when I decided to join Al-Anon to look at myself and my reaction to the alcoholics around me.

Al-Anon taught me that I was, in many ways, a little girl. I saw this especially in my angry times, when I could see myself acting out my frustrations to all the events that were out of my control when I was growing up. Al-Anon showed me I had tools to use at those times when I found someone else's behavior detrimental to my own. I know now how to detach and can detach even when my partner exhibits anger. Today I can learn to let go with the help of the program and the people in the program. Tomorrow I know I can continue to detach with love and confidence. I'm learning now that sometimes I have to do things that aren't the way I'd like them to be. But they're the way they need to be.

I'm also learning I need to show other people who I am. The little girl who looked out the window and vowed never to let anyone see how she felt is now ready to forget the pain of the past and look forward to the joy of the future. There will be times, I know, when I will be hurt and I'll want to close up. But I don't have to shut out the world at these times.

A.A. taught me how to get sober, but Al-Anon is now teaching me how to live without all the anchors and weights and chains of the past. Since coming to Al-Anon I've been able to make peace with my grandfather, although he had died before I was ready to do this. Despite the pain, I went back to my childhood and recalled the incident that caused me to lose the friendship I had with my grandfather. Al-Anon showed me I could make peace with him because I had learned how to be a lot more peaceful with myself.

I'm glad I forgave him. I've now regained the love I had for him when I was a child. There were some wonderful memories that I had with that man. Although I was sorry he had to drink, I learned more about the uncontrollability of the disease of alcoholism. I have accepted the disease and have been able to look at the person.

After I looked at my grandfather's illness, I had to look at my mother's illness. She is still an active alcoholic. Yet Al-Anon taught me how to let her be herself and to make her own choices. I love her despite the things I wish she didn't do. But I don't let her run my life and call the shots the way she used to. When she calls me up now and she's drunk, I terminate the conversation as quickly as I can — without anger or resentment toward her. I can love her for who she is, in spite of the disease she has.

I'm a very happy person today. I've got things in my life, people in my life, and a way of life I never thought could exist. I love my children and my partner dearly and have learned how to coexist with them through the beautiful tools of the program. Even though my mother — and now my brother — are both alcoholics, I can allow them to be who they are and accept them as they are. I no longer identify my behaviors with the ones of my grandfather and my mother. I'm a very different person from them. If my mother or brother called me tomorrow and said they needed my help, I'd be ready to say, "Can I take you to a meeting?" Today I'm my own person, but I'm ready whenever necessary to help someone else enjoy the health and sanity I now feel in my life.

TORN IN HALF

Gary's Story — Age: 25

Oh, what a tangled web do parents weave
When they think that their children are naive.

— *Ogden Nash*

For years I never fully realized anything had been wrong in my childhood. I only knew one thing: I thought I was going crazy. I felt different from everyone else. I couldn't seem to have close relationships with people. I didn't have many friends. None of my social relationships seemed to last longer than a few days or a few weeks. I felt insecure and unsure of myself both in social situations and on the job. I didn't really know what self-esteem was at that time, but I knew I lacked confidence in my abilities. I honestly didn't think I was very good at anything. I didn't believe anybody would need to come to me because of who I was as a person.

These are some of the reasons I was led to Adult Children of Alcoholics. In joining that fellowship, I had to confront the fact that I had grown up in an abusive and alcoholic household. To do so, I had to remember what it was like to grow up in a home where it was acceptable to be verbally and physically abused.

What once was . . .

One of my most vivid memories was of one of my father's alcoholic rampages when I was about nine or ten years old. My parents had been fighting, which usually happened whenever my father had been drinking. As their voices grew louder, their tone became more abusive. I was huddled in a room with the rest of the children, listening with fear and praying the fight wouldn't include me or my brothers and sisters.

Suddenly I started hearing louder noises and screaming. It sounded like someone was being killed. My mother had been a victim of father's temper many times, and she'd had the black eyes, bruises, and scratches to prove it. Now, I was afraid she was being hurt . . . no, I was actually afraid my father was doing what he had always threatened to do: kill her! I raced down the stairs to stop the fight.

When I came into the kitchen, I saw what had caused all the noise. My father had taken the entire six-chair kitchen set and reduced it to pieces of two-foot wood. He was screaming at my mother, who just stood there taking his abuse and not trying to stop him. I moved between them somehow, my ears ringing with the loud voices and my mother's sobs.

"Stop it, please stop it!" I think I yelled. "Stop hurting Mom!" At that interruption, my father focused his drunken attention upon me. He grabbed my arm in a rage. My mother tried to protect me and grabbed my other arm. They pulled at me from opposite sides. I remember seeing my father's face as he screamed: "Okay, so who do you love?"

That's how much of the abuse occurred in the family. My father would start drinking, he and my mother would start fighting, then he'd tire of her as a target and the kids would be involved. That's why my brothers and sisters would always hide as quickly as they could whenever fighting started. We felt like puppies, cowering under a bed or in the closet or whimpering in the corner until our angry master passed out or tired of his rampage.

I felt responsible for the safety and welfare of my family. I was the oldest boy of five children. I had an older sister, but I accepted at an early age the responsibility of being the "fixer" of the family. I was the one who comforted my brothers and sisters when they were crying or confused. I was the one who tried to pacify my father's temperamental mood swings. I'd do anything — absolutely anything — to keep peace in the house. Many times, I'd even go so far as to encourage my father's drinking. "Can I fix you a drink, Dad?" I'd ask, trying to distract his attention from abusing my mother or siblings. And I'd fix him that drink, because nine times out of ten it would keep the peace for a while.

I learned I had to be responsible because no one really stood up to my father. No one seemed to want to protect another. My mother offered us no protection whatsoever. In fact, she almost seemed supportive of my father's abusive behavior because she never left, she never stood up for herself, she never disagreed with him. When he became angry with her for having so many children, she would almost seem to agree with him, which told me she didn't really want me or my brothers or sisters around.

Even though I never fought back against my father's abuse, an incredible anger was growing inside me. The anger began to surface in many ways and at different times in my childhood. One of the first times occurred when I was of age for my church confirmation. Instead of blaming my father's drinking for the pain in my home, I felt an incredible anger at the supposedly benevolent God. I recall pointing an angry finger at God and blaming Him for everything. "How could You let this go on!" I screamed at God. How could I even acknowledge a belief in something so full of love and beauty if I saw none of that in my home life? I didn't even acknowledge there was a God. I rejected God. I flatly refused to be confirmed, with no explanation. My parents didn't question me. I wasn't confirmed.

When I wasn't feeling anger, I was filled with feelings of guilt or depression. My guilt would surface whenever my mother would abuse me emotionally with comments like, "Oh, you're just like your father." Or she would state her regrets out loud at having me and my brothers and sisters. Many times I felt like things would be so much better if I just weren't around.

That's when I began turning the anger inward. If my parents didn't want me around, maybe I could do something about that. I wanted to die. I started to starve myself. I ate less and less and lost weight. My parents finally noticed and made a doctor's appointment for me. The doctor took one look at me and told my parents my problem was psychological. So, off to a psychologist I went, along with my mother and father. But the first time the psychologist hinted the problem might have its root in the family, my father terminated the sessions.

I stopped the suicidal starvation, but continued to feel angry and miserable inside. Although I did fairly well in school, I didn't have many friends and felt very isolated. I believed I was a bad person, someone that nobody would want for a friend. I vividly remember being in grade school and desperately wanting to have friends and be invited to parties and sleep-overs. But I had a couple of counts against me. One was my bad feelings about myself, and the other was the fact that my family had a problem that was obvious to the rest of the neighborhood. It was foolish to think no one saw the police cars when they came to stop my parents' fighting. How could people in the neighborhood not hear the screaming and yelling and crying and hitting? How could they not see my mother's bruised and scratched face?

One of the most visible signs of my family's difference from the rest of the neighborhood was in the condition of our yard and house. Everyone else had a nice, neat, grassy lawn and a painted, repaired, cared for home. Our yard and home were a mess. My father hardly ever did any work around the yard at all. One day, thinking that if only we had a nice lawn, other kids would want to come over and play with me, I planted grass seed in a small area of the yard. My father yelled out to me, "Hey, you missed a spot over there," and went back to his drinking.

I had zero confidence in myself. I remember playing basketball with some guys and feeling rejected whenever they didn't pass the ball to me. That simple act bombarded me with negative voices that screamed in my head, "See, nobody thinks very much of you. If they did, they'd be passing that ball to you. But you're not good. You're no good."

Often when I did go out with friends in high school, the socializing revolved around drinking. We'd buy some liquor and go joyriding. I was always a willing passenger, a passive person who believed there wasn't much to do with people except drink. I had a difficult time socializing anyway, so the alcohol seemed to help me fit in to what everyone else was doing.

At this time in my life, my father wasn't around anymore. He and my mother had gotten a divorce when I was fifteen. At first I thought his moving out of the house would be a good thing for the family, but I soon learned my father was going to be there very much in spirit. My mother, who also had been affected by the disease of alcoholism, began dating men who also had substance abuse problems. They were drinkers or drug users who expressed their emotions with the same angry intensity as my father had.

I remember vividly the relationship she had with one man. He had an incredible temper, but up to that point I had only heard and seen him abuse my mother. When I came home from school one day, I learned he had hit one of my sisters in the face with his workboot. That's when my anger finally boiled to the surface.

I belonged to a sportsman's club and had access to guns. One night, I took one and hid it inside my jacket. I felt entirely overcome by an anger that was finally going to be expressed in a gunshot at a man I hated. Except this man wasn't just my mother's boyfriend. He represented my father and all the other men who had come into the house and abused the family after my dad had left.

I remember my mother met me that night at the top of the stairs. She must have been warned by some look in my eyes, because she suddenly seemed to know what was on my mind. I stopped and looked at her, and I lost my nerve. The rest of that night is lost in a foggy memory, but I do know I never used the gun. I know now, looking back, how badly I wanted to end the horrible life I was living in. I just didn't know at the time how I was going to escape it or how my brothers and sisters were going to escape it.

But escape it I finally did, in the way most kids do. I left home and went to college. I was so glad to be out of the house. I couldn't wait until I got out of college and was really out living on my own, in my own job and living space. I still didn't know who I was or what I wanted from life, but I did know I didn't want anything my parents had. That kind of a life wasn't for me.

What is now . . .

But I didn't know how to change my life. I just didn't have the tools to suddenly get out in the "real" world and be a normal person. Looking back at the time shortly before I got involved in the Adult Children of Alcoholics program, I knew I was really, really messed up. It wasn't like I was suicidal or anything. I was depressed, but I didn't know why. I felt horrible about myself, and I didn't know why. I remember telling myself how proud I should be of going to college and graduating and getting a good job, but I couldn't seem to feel good about anything I did on the inside.

On the outside, I don't think it looked like I had a problem at all. But if you took a look inside, you would've found a lonely, unhappy man.

Living outside of the home was very little help to me, because I began to relive my childhood over and over in my mind. I'd lie wide awake in bed until all hours, hearing the angry voices and abuse like a tape recorder that couldn't shut off. I knew I'd have to do something soon, because I really felt like I was going crazy.

I made an appointment with a therapist, but cancelled it. I made another and another, but cancelled them both. Finally, on my fourth attempt, I made it into the therapist's office.

I will forever be grateful to this counselor to have had the training to help me deal with the fact that I was from an alcoholic home. But beyond that, he told me to go to Adult Children of Alcoholics meetings. It's one thing to sit in a therapist's office and recall the details of an alcoholic background. It's another to go to meetings where you're surrounded by those who share, not only similar background experiences, but the same feelings.

I remember the first time I walked into an ACOA meeting. I listened to the people talking and had a strange sensation they were all there talking about me. I began to get nervous. What they were saying was hitting close — very close — to home.

Finally, during the last few minutes of the meeting, I raised my hand. I don't really remember what I said. I believe I introduced myself and just said I related to everything that everyone had said. But what I didn't say was how relieved I felt inside. I wanted to cry out, "Thank God I've found somewhere to go so I can live!"

ACOA meetings and the information I gather from them affect everything in my life: how I feel about myself, how I view myself in my career, how I set limits and goals in my life.

One area where ACOA has been truly beneficial is my career. Before I had the program in my life, I would be a tireless "giver" on the job. I would never be honest about my limitations. If someone wanted me to do a project and someone else wanted me to do another, I couldn't seem to say no to either one. So I'd take on both projects and work my tail off to get them done perfectly and on time for both the people. I was afraid if I didn't they wouldn't like me or I'd lose my job.

If my boss gave me a great deal of responsibility on a special assignment, I'd run into him almost every step of the way to check that everything I was doing was right. I didn't have any confidence in me or my abilities, and I couldn't understand why he trusted me to get a certain assignment done. Even when he'd tell me to make my own decisions, I would feel helpless and directionless unless he was there to give me continual support.

Now I use the program on the job, and it has helped tremendously. I think one of my proudest moments came when someone requested my help on a project. I had never refused that person before, and I had certainly acquired the reputation of being an easy pushover. I told this person I couldn't do the project for him since I had other more important things that took priority. It felt so good to be able to set my limits and to not feel I had lost his approval because of what I said.

The program has taught me that there is only one thing that is important to me: ME! I'm learning how to take care of myself through the many tools of the program. At meetings, people listen to me and offer wonderful guidance and their experience in handling similar situations in their lives. I use the slogans to remember my growth will come through working the program *One Day at a Time*, gently and lovingly. I am learning how to make and keep friends through the program. I'm learning who Gary is for the first time in my life, and I'm beginning to like him!

What can be . . .

I have a great deal of hope for my future. That feels so good to say, considering how hopeless and despairing I felt for so many years.

I think I owe many of my hopeful feelings to the faith I now am beginning to have in a Power greater than myself. I learned in ACOA I am powerless over alcohol but I do have power over my life and how I want to live it. I don't want to be overresponsible any more, and that's why I truly believe there is a Power greater than myself that can restore me to sanity. I now rarely feel I'm going crazy. When I do have those feelings, I'm able to let them go, pray, and trust all will be well if I only believe I am well. Every day my faith grows stronger, and therefore I become stronger.

I see the future in my career as being very bright and positive. I see myself being able to believe in my boss's trust in my abilities. I know I can become more willing to function independently when I need to. By working the program and becoming stronger, I see myself taking more risks and greater responsibilities.

I enjoy my job so much more now that I've learned how to set my limits. I'm no longer burned out from trying to satisfy everyone else's needs. When I feel tired from long hours on the job, it's a good kind of tired feeling. I'm pleased with my work, my efforts, and the dedication I've been able to show.

My personal relationships are getting better too. I know each day I'll find it easier to communicate my needs and feelings. Going to meetings on a regular basis helps me, because there I hear other people talking about their vulnerabilities and sharing their feelings. By listening to others take risks, I know I can too.

My family life still affects me from time to time, but the influences aren't as strong and don't last as long as they used to. I know now I can't fix or save my family. The children are on their own now, trying to cope in an intense world with feelings left over from an intense childhood. When I entered ACOA, not one of my brothers or sisters wanted to be involved. Recently, one of my sisters attended her first meeting. That felt so good, because it was the first time I was asked to chair a meeting and tell my story. She was crying during the meeting, but I didn't try to take care of her like I would have in the past. I let the room full of caring, supporting, and understanding people go to her and let her feel what I felt when I attended my first meeting. She's been back a couple of times since then, although the meetings aren't easy for her. She still has many painful feelings and is very afraid to feel them.

I have hope for my family. My mother has become quite curious about the wonderful changes in me and has asked many questions about ACOA. Once she told me she might like to come to a meeting. She now realizes that she, too, grew up in an alcoholic home. Once I knew that, I began to have more understanding for her behavior when I was growing up. I've learned, through ACOA, that many adult children form relationships with alcoholics because they have personalities similar to those they grew up with. That certainly seemed to be my mother's pattern.

My father continues to drink. When I got into ACOA, I wanted to run to him and save him from his disease. Now I know I am powerless over his behavior. He needs to come to his own conclusions or reach bottom in his own time. I see him occasionally, but it's very difficult. When my sister gave birth to her first baby, he showed up at the hospital drunk. When I visit him now at his apartment, he has a difficult time looking me in the eye or even standing close to me. Our conversations are often short. Many times he walks around his apartment or keeps his back turned to me.

I do have compassion for him. I do have understanding of his problem. I have forgiven him for his past behaviors. What the program gives me is the courage to tell him how I feel, but the wisdom to know he needs to find himself in his own time and in his own way. But when he does find his way, I know I can be there for him.

ADDICTED TO EXCITEMENT

Betsy's story — Age 45

All a child's life depends on the ideal it has of its parents. . . . Absolute trust in someone else is the essence of education.

— E. M. *Forster*

I don't have much recollection of what went on in my home when I was growing up. Incidents come back to me now in bits and pieces, with no real continuity. I do have a good memory, however, about what it felt like to grow up in an alcoholic home. There were two distinct feelings — tension and fear.

As I was growing up, I dealt with those feelings by seeking out exciting people and unhealthy situations. By adulthood, however, I found I had become addicted to excitement and to very unhealthy people. I was like a junkie searching for a fix, going from one crisis situation to the next. Whenever life was calm and serene for me, I felt depressed. Whenever life was turned upside down, I felt comfortable.

My career as an addictions therapist helped me ignore my own addiction: I focused obsessively on my patients' problems. But then I became emotionally, physically, and spiritually addicted to a very unhealthy person. Suddenly things weren't so exciting anymore. In fact, I felt I was losing control. That's when I had to get help from another member of my profession and confront what I had avoided facing all my life — that I was the child of an alcoholic. Along with this truth, I discovered I was a very untrusting and fearful person, especially in intimate relationships. That fear, I knew, had been learned from my alcoholic father, as well as my codependent mother.

What once was . . .

I grew up in a well-to-do neighborhood with my mother, my father, and my younger brother. From the outside, our family appeared normal. My father was a successful businessman who rarely missed a day of work. We lived in a nice Colonial home, had two cars, and owned just about every nice thing that money could buy.

57

That was from the outside, looking in. From the inside, looking out, things felt very, very wrong at my house. I could never put my finger on a reason. Nothing was visible; there seemed to be no problem. But there seemed to be an uncomfortable feeling that filled the house like a cancer. That feeling made my stomach churn in knots and made me yearn to get out of the house as much as possible.

When I'd spend time at friends' houses, I'd see differences between the behaviors in their homes and those behaviors in mine. The one main difference would be the way the families interacted with one another. They seemed to talk to each other a lot, sometimes even loudly, to get their points across. That was never allowed in my house.

My father was authoritarian. What he said could never, ever be contradicted. In our house, voices were never raised and arguments never happened. There could be no disputing my father's rule.

We dealt with his dictatorship in individual ways. My mother internalized all her feelings. As a result, she ended up with severe stomach problems. Most of my memories of my mother focus around her daily vomiting sessions in the bathroom. By the time I was in high school, she had had nearly two-thirds of her stomach removed.

My brother was pretty much buffered from the force of my father's autocracy because he was the favorite of the family. Plus, he was younger. So I was the child who felt most of my father's unbudging personality. There were times with him that could be good, like when we'd go for walks in the snow or play Ping-Pong. But most of the time I was utterly confused and fearful around my father.

I didn't know what was causing my father's strange behavior. The more I observed him, however, the more I mistakenly came to believe he was mentally ill. Once I reached this diagnosis, I acted very cautiously around him. I would never try to contradict him. Mostly I would endure him and just get through his tirades until I could leave and go to my room.

But there were times that, no matter what I did, I would suddenly find myself embroiled in a "reprimand session." I hated those sessions. He would make me sit at the kitchen table; then he'd embark on a lengthy lecture. My role was to sit still and listen to whatever he had to say until he was finished. I usually had no idea why I was there.

Sometimes I'd try really hard to listen to what he was saying so I could figure out what I had done wrong and not do it again. But he'd start his sentences one way, then end them up in a totally different way. He'd contradict himself until my head would be swimming. I finally gave up trying to figure out the reasons behind those sessions and attributed them all to his mental illness. I would, therefore, sit quietly at the table and listen to him go on and on.

As a result of my father's crazy behaviors, I grew up terrified of him without his ever laying a hand on me. He exuded an aura of such tension and anger and contradiction that I couldn't trust him at all. I never knew when he would act nice and when he would act strange. So I'd walk around the house on eggshells and try not to get in his way.

At one point my fear of him and my inner tension grew so overpowering that I worked out a way not to see him for almost six months — even though he came home every day! If I was downstairs and saw him coming in the house, I'd rush up to my room and close the door. If I was up in my room and heard him coming to check on me, I'd lie down in bed and pretend I was asleep. For those six months, I didn't have to go through one lecture. It was wonderful!

The happiest times for me were the days between June and September when my family and relatives rented and shared two cottages by the ocean. I loved that time for many reasons. One was that I rarely had any negative interactions with my father. With all the people around us, he became a little less authoritarian. I also had more freedom to run around, play with my cousins, and visit with my aunts and uncles. I was fortunate to have such a loving extended family, for it felt like I could be myself during those summer months — happy and relaxed.

Looking back today, I can get some clues about the denial of sickness in my family. The first clue was that my father never wanted us to tell anyone about a sickness or death in the family. He wanted our family to appear fine from the outside, even if we were miserable on the inside. As a result, no one knew about my mother's stomach problems or the fact that I had been hospitalized for a serious illness when I was growing up.

The second clue was in the lying I heard. I remember one time listening to my mother say into the telephone, "I'm sorry, but he's not here. " I could see my father sitting right there in the living room across from her. I remember my confusion. Why would she lie about the fact that my father was right there not five feet from her? Now, of course, I realize he was probably three sheets to the wind and she was covering up for him.

Knowing what I know now about the roles children play in the alcoholic home, I can honestly say I tried very hard to be the family hero. I always wanted to do the right thing and achieve the best. But I was usually made into the scapegoat. My brother came off as the family hero without even trying. No matter what I did, it was always wrong. Yet no matter what my brother did, it was always good. He was given far more emotional and financial consideration than I was, both as a child and as an adult. As a result, I grew up resenting my brother.

I gave up trying to be the family hero when I learned nothing I did would ever be good enough. Instead, I started finding happiness in other ways. I began to disobey my parents a lot and caused problems in school with my friends.

In high school, I was always in the "in" group and, although I wasn't the most popular, I was usually the close friend to the most popular person. Because I was Jewish, my parents didn't want me dating or hanging out with people who weren't Jewish. So what did I do? I hung out and dated all the kids they never would have approved of! Whenever I was put in charge of babysitting my brother, my parents would give me strict orders: "No one over here and no parties. " So I'd be sure to invite as many people over as I could.

One night I had to babysit my brother. Naturally I had invited a lot of my friends over. We all were out in the backyard playing softball when my brother was hit accidentally by a bat. He started bleeding, so I knew I'd have to take him to the hospital. My brother and I and all the people I wasn't supposed to have over to my house went to the local emergency room. I was having a ball — such excitement! But even better than that was the look on my parents' faces when they saw my black friends in the emergency room.

I loved doing exciting things like that. I loved walking that thin line and being rebellious. In my senior year I skipped 45 days. When the administration found out my friends and I were planning a huge senior party, they decided that anyone caught at that party wouldn't be able to graduate. They called five families to warn them of that decision. My parents were one of the five. They were somewhat upset, but not as upset as I was that I couldn't go.

I left home as soon as I graduated. My parents wanted me to go to school, then work in a hospital and marry a doctor. I decided to be a social worker and married an unemployed truck driver.

I finally realized my father had a drinking problem after I was married, but my husband had to point it out to me. He and I were driving home after attending a family dinner party. While we had been sitting at the dinner table, my father had been acting very strange and talking nonsense. On the way home, I said to my husband, "I think my father is mentally ill."

"Why do you say that?" he asked.

"Didn't you hear him at the dinner table? He wasn't making any sense. You couldn't understand half his words because he was slurring so badly!"

My husband laughed. "He was drunk, for crying out loud. Anybody could see that!"

Never before had I realized my father was a drinker and those were the effects of alcohol. Now I knew. But I didn't put two and two together about my childhood then.

Some years into my marriage, I started feeling bored and began doing volunteer social work. My first job was working with chemically dependent people. I had no problem working with drug addicts, but I refused to work with alcoholics. I didn't know why I was so adamant about not working with them, but my boss respected my wishes. The volunteer work soon became a full-time job.

At about this time, my daughter and I went with my parents to a bar mitzvah. My father became drunk. He couldn't stand up. He dropped food on the floor and on himself. Mercifully, the evening came to a close. My father insisted on driving, and we began a wrestling match for the car keys. I finally took them from him and drove everyone home. When we got there, he immediately passed out in bed. I started to go upstairs too, but my mother stopped me. For the first time, she had an open and honest conversation with me. She told me how upset she was about my father's drinking and how he had been drinking long before I had been born. She said she didn't know what she was going to do anymore. She was at the end of her rope and was begging me for help.

Knowing what I knew from my job, I told her about Al-Anon and suggested she try it. Six months into the program, she felt she was "cured." She had listened at the meetings and learned alcoholism was a disease. Since she knew my father couldn't stop drinking, she decided to accept him as an incurable alcoholic. He continued to drink, and she stopped attending meetings.

The night my mother talked to me created some chinks in my denial armor. I couldn't sleep. All the feelings I had had as a child came back to me. I remembered the tension, the fear, and the nightmares. I made a decision not to feel that pain anymore. I avoided contact with my parents for two years and buried myself in my work, trying hard not to feel any emotions.

I loved working with the junkies in my job. I would work 60 to 80 hours a week and still not seem to get enough. Many times they would ask me if I was a recovering addict. They were convinced drugs were my addiction, but little did they know how addicted I was to the addicts themselves. They were exciting people. They all had a lot of problems — emotional and physical. I was addicted to the excitement of their lives and personalities, and I couldn't get enough of them.

I was never happier than when I'd have to "hide out" someone in my home from an abuser or take a suicide call in the middle of the night. Many of my co-workers called me "Crusader Rabbit," because I really was out to save those people. For the seven years I ran a drug program in the local jail, I was on a high just with the excitement of that job.

But the wonderful high soon crashed to a horrible low. I became involved with a drug addict. This involvement soon turned into an addiction. I couldn't see this man enough. I hated being separated from him. I felt controlled by him and the feelings I had for him. I started to act like a person possessed. My husband found out about the relationship and threw me out of the house.

Finally, I made the decision to go to a therapist. I felt things were really getting out of hand. I needed some help.

What is now . . .

My therapist helped me truly see and accept that there had been alcohol in my childhood. But that occurred only after a great deal of work on her part. It was incredible, the amount of denial I had developed. I can recall saying to her, "I think my father is a little alcoholic, but I don't think he's *that* alcoholic. "

For two years she worked with me, trying to convince me to get into a treatment program for families of alcoholics. All that time I continued to work as the director of a crisis hotline. I was still deeply hooked into the addictive relationship with the drug addict. My life became crazier and crazier.

Finally, my life got so unbearable I signed up for the week-long family program. That was three years ago. From there I went directly into the Al-Anon and ACOA (Adult Children of Alcoholics) Twelve Step program. My life has never been the same since.

The first time I walked into an ACOA meeting, I felt I had arrived in the right place. It was as if a 500-pound weight had been lifted from my shoulders.

One statement made at that meeting seemed to touch me deeply and take away many of the anxious feelings I had inside. That statement was simple: When you grow up in an alcoholic home, you don't know what normal is. What a sense of relief I had from that statement! Now I no longer had to think I was crazy. Much of that craziness was based on the contradictory feelings I had about myself.

For instance, I believed I was in the height of my career. I was making some great achievements and receiving a great deal of recognition for the work I was doing. People knew me and respected me. My name was seen in the local and county papers. I was asked to speak to community groups and schools. I was interviewed for television talk shows. Despite these wonderful, positive career strokes, I didn't know which end was up. I felt totally out of touch with who I was and where I was going.

That first ACOA meeting soothed my anxious feelings by letting me know it was okay to be confused. I learned most adult children grow up with similar feelings. I also learned I hadn't caused that confusion. That confusion, I discovered, was a result of how I had learned to cope as a child in an alcoholic home.

I hadn't been in the program too long before I started to make some really positive changes in my life. The first related to my job. When I made my career choice as a social worker, I thought I was doing it for all the right reasons. But as I became healthier in the program, I soon realized I had chosen the profession for all the wrong reasons

I used my career as a way of making me feel good, making me feel needed, making me feel worthwhile. I desperately needed a job to give me those feelings because I didn't know how to get any of them on my own.

My work in the program helped me realize just how crazy that job was making me. After a good deal of soul-searching and talking with people in the program, I quit my social work job after nearly a decade of rescuing others.

The second thing I did was break off my addictive relationship. That certainly wasn't easy. In fact, I think it was one of the most difficult things I had to do. But I didn't do it alone. I asked my sponsor to be with me, and she helped me look at how I needed to help myself, not someone else. She made me realize just how much I had been using that relationship to provide for needs that I really needed to learn to satisfy on my own.

The third thing I did was confront my father on an issue that really bothered me. Ever since I had been a child, my father had always equated money with love and affection. He would shower this money on my brother, yet blatantly seemed to deny me.

When my marriage was breaking up, my father called me to say he would help me financially in any way he could. I had heard that promise before, but for some reason I believed him this time. So when my lawyer told me I had to come up with several hundred dollars during the divorce proceedings, I called my father to accept his help. He refused to give me any money. I was furious!

My therapist recommended a confrontation. I was so nervous. How could I possibly confront my father? I needed a great deal of courage to accept the challenge of standing up to a man I had always backed down to. I made plans to stay with my parents for the weekend. Then I waited until early morning to talk with my father, when I was pretty much assured he wouldn't be drunk. I went into his bedroom and faced him as he sat on the bed.

I said, "You know, you have a tendency sometimes to say things that you'll do. You make promises to me. Then when I take you up on those promises, you refuse me. It's really confusing to me and I'd really appreciate it if you just didn't offer at all unless you mean it."

He sat on the bed with a weird look on his face, looking at me. Then he started rocking back and forth on the bed like a baby.

Suddenly he started screaming, "That's it! You're cut out of the will!" He continued to scream and yell at me for the rest of the day, until I left for home.

I learned confrontation isn't appropriate for me with an alcoholic like my father. I also came in touch with how sick he was. For as long as alcohol runs his life, I know I'll have a difficult time opening honest communication channels between us.

What can be . . .

One of the tools of the program I've used constantly from the beginning is a sponsor. To me, a sponsor is almost as important to working the program as the Twelve Steps are. I have done most of my work with my sponsor. One of my biggest issues is trust. With that trust comes a fear of intimacy and a fear of showing love to another, whether it's a man or a woman. In my position as therapist, I am often seen as an authority figure and as someone who is "together." In such a position of autonomy, it was easy for me to forget I have feelings and needs and vulnerabilities that have to be developed and shown.

In my sponsor, I have a fellow human being with whom I can show my feelings and needs and vulnerabilities. This sponsor has turned out to be the first person I've ever trusted totally. With her, I can say I'm feeling lousy and know it's okay to feel that way.

As we grew to know each other, we decided to become each other's sponsors because we were both so helpful to one another. I find it's a relationship that works out well and really helps me to trust. I have the courage to be a lot more open because she is open with me. It's better than two friends saying to each other, "Oh, you'll be all right in the morning. You'll get over it." Together, we work on finding ways to deal with difficult situations and confusing feelings.

With this trust, I find other areas in my life are improving. The first area is my career. I'm now in a different job, without the intensity of the prison rehab issues. Granted, my job doesn't have all the excitement of the past, but it has everything I need for me. Now I'm not working for people anymore. I'm not there 100 percent of the time for sick, needy people. Now I'm doing my job because I *want* to, not because I need to for my self-esteem. Today I'm better at setting limits. Now I know when I can't listen to someone else's problems because I need help with my own.

My barriers are starting to come down. I'm getting used to telling people how I really feel, not what I think they want to hear. Recently a close friend killed herself. At first I felt responsible for her death. But, over time and through the health and help of the program, I've learned not to blame myself. I couldn't rescue her. I can't rescue anybody. I can only rescue myself.

Sometimes I wish my old fixes would work for me, because they usually were able to take me away from my depression and pain. Sometimes I think of Peggy Lee's song, "Is That All There Is?" and wonder how much I really do like serenity.

But I do have hope for the future. I do have faith that I'll be able to be more trusting of people and unafraid of showing love. Someday I want to be involved in an intimate relationship without feeling fear and distrust. Today I can't say I'm ready, but who knows what's in store for me? With all the growing I've done so far in the program, I know my movement toward happiness and contentment is only a question of time.

NO MEMORIES OF MEMORIES

David's Story — Age: 42

Don't you think that everyone looks back on their childhood with a certain amount of regret about something?

— *Ernest Thompson*

There's not very much I remember about my childhood. I have no significant memories of it being bad. I guess I grew up believing everything was fine. I wasn't ecstatically happy, but I chose not to deal with anything that made me feel otherwise.

Adulthood wasn't easy for me. I had difficulty maintaining relationships and steady jobs. I had first a drinking and then a drug problem. It was only when I entered the Twelve Step programs of Alcoholics Anonymous and Narcotics Anonymous that significant changes started to occur. I also joined Adult Children of Alcoholics at the same time, because I was into fixing myself and felt ACOA couldn't hurt me.

What happened in those ACOA meetings was I started to think about my childhood. It was very difficult for me to look back at the negative things that had happened to me. All I could seem to want to hold on to were the positive times. Anything beyond that I wanted to deny and say weren't really all that bad or didn't matter to me.

But every time I attended another ACOA meeting, I started to remember a little bit more from my past. I started to get in touch with my feelings and became more honest with the fact that my feelings were — and still are — difficult to feel. Bit by bit, I'm starting to remember what it was like for me to grow up in an alcoholic home.

What once was . . .

I have two versions of what it was like for me to grow up. In the first version, I glance back quickly at my past and say, "I had a *great* childhood!" I remember myself in this version being pretty happy as a kid. I see myself being connected with a lot of good friends. I recall being a neat guy, so I ended up having neat friends.

I remember doing things like swimming a lot and going out and doing things with a number of people. I was pretty independent. I had a sense of self-esteem.

There's another version of my childhood that I've only just started to look at. This version isn't really in my head as clearly as the first. It's kind of fuzzy, so it relies heavily upon what one of my two older sisters said when she described what I looked like as a kid: "You used to hang around the house a lot and look sad."

When I start to get in touch with that sadness, then I start to remember some of the things that occurred in my childhood that weren't so happy. That's the second, more truthful version. . . .

Both of my parents were alcoholics throughout my childhood. I remember seeing bottles of liquor around the house when I was young, but I never thought much about it. I thought every house had bottles of liquor around. It wasn't until I was in my late teens that I started to notice alcohol affected my parents in a negative way.

Until that time, I didn't really notice my parents a lot. I never really had a relationship with either one of them. When I was a baby I had a nanny who took care of me. I was told my parents were very prominent and did a great deal of socializing, which was confirmed by the photographs and newspaper clippings I saw. My father never took me to baseball games or football games. Friends of the family would always be appointed for those duties. I don't ever remember doing anything with my mother. Sometimes I wonder where my parents were when I was growing up.

There was very little stability in my life while I was growing up. In the first version of my childhood — the happy one — I remember being surrounded by friends all the time. But those friendships didn't last very long because we were always moving. My parents would buy a house, fix it up, sell it; buy another, fix it up, sell it; and so on. In my entire childhood, I moved no less than fifteen times. With each move, I'd get a new bunch of friends. The friends I had left behind would soon be forgotten.

At first I adapted pretty well to the constant packing and moving, packing and moving routine. It became easy for me to let go of old friends and start making new ones. It seemed okay that nothing was really settled, stable, or permanent.

But the last move was most difficult for me, because that's when I started to be in touch with the patterns that occurred in my life. I was sixteen years old when my dad came home from work one evening and announced, "Okay, I'm being transferred. Let's go to Idaho." Once again I had to move.

While we were in Idaho I became aware of the drinking in my parents' lives. I was now also overhearing their arguments. These arguments became louder and more vicious as their drinking continued.

They would start to drink their cocktails the minute my father came home from work. The only thing that could interrupt their cocktail hours would be arguments over money. This last move found my parents pretty broke and in debt. They would therefore argue constantly over any money issue.

Their alcohol consumption escalated. They started associating with a much younger crowd. They partied frequently. They drank every night. And argued and argued.

Their life together wasn't working out the way they wanted it to. They were miserable with themselves and with each other. They carried this misery into everything they did.

I started to be miserable about things too. I kept hanging around my drunken parents, even though I was eighteen years old and could have easily left on my own. But I didn't leave them when we were in Idaho, and I continued to stay with them when they were transferred back to the East.

Their daily drinking continued. Their arguments grew more vicious and vocal. They started screaming about "whose fault it was." It was never clear to me, when I overheard their arguments, what the "it" was and why it mattered who was at "fault."

But what I did hear was them blaming my sisters or me. They started to trace all of their problems back to the kids. I felt guilty when I overheard those statements, but all I could say to myself was, "Then why don't you get out of here?" I didn't stop living with my parents until I was in my early 30s even though I was miserable at home. I was also pretty miserable with myself and my life. I wasn't doing very much besides being a ski bum and a heavy drinker.

I didn't have very many skills to fall back on. I had never been a very good student. My parents dealt with that at first by getting me a tutor, but I hated those sessions. There was always some other neighborhood kid with me who knew more than I did. The tutor would invariably say to the smarter kid, "Now, tell David what the answer is." I felt really stupid.

I never got beyond my freshman year of high school. I flunked out my first go-round, tried again, but never stuck with it. I then joined the Coast Guard to get a quick education and try to do something with my life. After 22 days, I was honorably discharged and sent home.

I kept busy moving from job to job and trying to be the peace keeper at home. Right before I left, there was a lot of fighting and very heavy drinking. My father was a dying man with his alcoholism and stress. My mother became mentally ill and increasingly unable to cope.

I left home with a drinking problem, a reputation for instability in jobs and relationships, and no significant tools for coping with the world.

What is now . . .
When I was 29 years old I put myself in detox for five days to try to stop drinking. Two days after that, I was out drinking again. I received some therapy and got in touch with a treatment center that had a month-long program for alcoholics. I stayed for two weeks.

But when I left there, I stopped drinking for good. I started drugs the minute I quit drinking, going from one crutch to the next. Pot became my daily drug of choice. I became very obsessed about having my drug every day. I was hooked.

I also became obsessed with a friend's daughter who was significantly younger than me. I used her as a crutch and we lived together for a couple of years. But then she decided to go overseas and live. She left, and I went right to the bottom.

When a therapist told me I should start going to some Twelve Step meetings, I figured I might as well. I had nowhere else to go. I joined Narcotics Anonymous, then Alcoholics Anonymous. When I heard about Adult Children of Alcoholics, I decided to try that too.

The first ACOA meeting was very powerful for me indeed. In fact, it was probably the most emotional thing I've ever experienced. Up until that meeting, I had tried all kinds of therapies for getting in touch with my emotions and body. But none of them hit me the way the ACOA meeting did. I could actually feel physical bodily shifts inside of me — in my chest, my head, all over my body. The shifts called out to me, "These are your problems, David. This is who you are."

I went to that first meeting blind, not knowing what to expect. But I had many questions from my childhood answered in that one meeting, and I kept going back.

I started thinking about my past. As I did, I discovered that I held a very significant belief: that every day of my life, up until that day I walked into ACOA, I was a child. From that day on, it was up to me to use the meetings to discover how I could start to live my life as an adult.

70

What can be . . .

It's still hard for me to think negative feelings towards my parents and how they raised me. I look at their lives and realize how miserable they were. My father died at the age of 62 of alcoholism and stress. His drinking had been continuous through several heart attacks and a bad fall. By that time he was no longer just an evening drinker. He was drinking on weekend mornings and coming home from work with the smell of liquor on his breath.

My mother's mental illness became evident when my father died. She has had many opportunities to become independent since his death, but she has chosen to live dependently and helplessly in a nursing home.

Through ACOA, I've been able to forgive both of them for the past they gave me. I see now they had no control over themselves, the way they lived, or their disease.

Once I forgave my parents, I was able to learn a great deal about myself in the program. As much as I'd like to believe that ACOA is filled with profound pearls of wisdom, it's really quite simple. All it requires is to attend meetings, listen, and share with others.

For the first few meetings I was uncomfortable with the way people were in touch with their feelings. They could talk about their emotions and past problems quite openly. But now I see the group as a family, a bunch of very together people who can talk about what's wrong with them while, at the same time, they learn how to feel good about themselves.

Part of feeling good about me is being able to understand and accept I did have a past. When I first listened to people talk about their childhoods, I believed they had more problems than I had. I felt maybe I shouldn't be in ACOA if I had only a few problems compared to someone else's many.

But now I know my life was no piece of cake either. I belong to ACOA because my childhood wasn't what it should have been. I had two alcoholic parents who were incapable of taking care of themselves, let alone another human being. They therefore could give me no tools with which to build my life.

Today the ACOA program gives me the tools I need to build my life skills. One of those skills is learning how to become a responsible person. In my steady job, I am now a much better worker. I'm more attentive to the people and the materials.

Another life skill is being able to maintain and grow in an intimate relationship. I am involved in a relationship that I didn't think I could possibly have because of my low self-esteem. But I'm learning now, in this relationship, that I can be capable of meeting someone else's needs as well as communicate my own. Talking about feelings is one of the better parts of this relationship, as well as dealing with the issues of the relationship in a responsible and mature manner. It's not easy all the time, but I know that's okay because today I have some tools that make it easier.

Bit by bit, my childhood memories are coming into focus. I'm able to actually talk about what it was like for me to grow up in an alcoholic home. I have some memories about the young David and how he felt while he was growing up. Recently I told my story in a meeting and was able to relate a past occurrence that had caused me a great deal of pain at the time. I had never before shared that incident with anyone else, let alone a roomful of people.

But the people in the meeting understood my feelings. And just by telling that one incident, I've let go of another painful part of my past. My life — and my past — have come together so much over the past year.

Finally, at the age of 42, I'm growing up. It feels great!

ADDICTED TO RELATIONSHIPS

Adrienne's Story — Age: 39

Many of us have a brokenhearted child within us. . . . The triumph of adult-hood is to heal that child.

— *Marlo Thomas*

My father was the alcoholic in my life. While I was growing up, he gave me inconsistent messages about our father-daughter relationship. One minute he'd be very loving with me, and we'd share some very special times. But that only happened when we were alone. If anyone else was around, he'd treat me like I didn't matter at all.

I was in high school when I started to identify an attraction toward women. I didn't act on that feeling until a woman showed an interest in me first. Then I felt special. She became my first relationship, and I left home to live with her. I thought that relationship was going to last forever, but when it ended, I quickly got into another. My life seemed to have meaning only when I was involved with someone. If that ended, I felt like I ended.

It wasn't until I recognized my father's drinking problems and confronted my own that I was able to see a pattern in my relationships. Then I was also able to recognize just how much of my life had focused on another person's needs rather than my own. Through ACOA, I learned I wasn't the only one who was addicted to relationships. I also learned I had to start focusing on myself, or I would never stop the steady stream of relationships that flowed in and out of my life.

What once was . . .

I grew up feeling very confused about relationships in my family. The person who confused me the most was my father. He was an alcoholic who began drinking heavily when I was eleven or twelve years old. I remember he had quit smoking at the time, saved up a lot of money, and bought himself a boat. He started to do a lot of drinking.

Drinking would change his personality. He would become very friendly and much nicer. Without the alcohol, he was a very angry man. He was a bear who would swing first and ask questions later. He was grouchy and we were afraid of him, as were our friends in the neighborhood.

My father took a great deal of his physical anger out on my older brother; then my brother would take it out on me. Like a chain reaction, I'd feel his anger follow down the line.

When my brother left home after high school to join the service, I was relieved to think the abuse would stop. But instead, my father started verbally abusing me and threatening violence. Suddenly I knew what my older brother had felt, and I yelled out to my father, "I'm not going to take this! I'm not going to be my brother for you now. " With that, my father backed off.

I was still afraid of him. I always had a sense of impending doom whenever he was around. I tiptoed around him and tried to stay away from him as much as possible, not only to avoid the anger but also because of the embarrassment I felt whenever he was drunk. He'd open his mouth and talk gibberish. If you asked him what he said, he'd switch everything around and say, "Well, that's what I meant to say. " I never could translate what he was saying when he was drunk.

My father didn't always have those negative behaviors. There were times I really enjoyed him and had a good time with him. He could be nice to me, but only when we were alone. Those times with him were so special to me, because I got to see him in a different light. I loved the man he was then, because he could be my buddy. He showed me then that I meant something to him. In many ways, he treated me like a son, teaching me things and sharing them with me.

Summers with my father at our cottage were especially nice because we'd get to spend a lot of time alone. My brother and older sister had summer jobs, so they had to stay at home during the week with my mother. That meant I could go down to the cottage with my father and take care of him by cooking his meals and such. But he would always end up taking care of me. He was sweet and pleasant, and we did many things together, like fix up the cottage and fish and be buddy-buddy with each other.

When my mother and sister and brother would come down during the weekends, he'd explode. Having other people around just seemed to set him off. That was very confusing for me, because I'd keep talking to him and acting like I had been when I was with him all week. But he'd act as though the week had never happened. He'd yell at me a lot and act as if I didn't matter.

During times like that, I would feel very confused and alone. I'd also feel like I wasn't wanted. That wasn't an unfamiliar feeling to me because I also felt the same way at home. Then one time my father was drunk, and he told me that I was an accident. I remember when he told me that I just shrugged it off and said, "I knew that." But inside I was crushed. By his statement, he had confirmed my suspicions that they didn't really want me.

People saw me as a shy and frightened little girl. Because I believed nobody really cared about me, I was uncomfortable around people. The friends I did have were usually boys and younger than I. I felt more comfortable with younger people than with people my own age or older. I guess I felt more sure of myself if I was the older one.

I had a great deal of trouble in school that related to my shyness. I was picked on by kids as well as teachers. One teacher called my mother into school because she thought I was too quiet. She believed I was emotionally disturbed. Another teacher called me a dummy. I think she was trying to motivate me to try harder, but that only made me feel worse.

I felt pretty badly about myself. At school, as well as at home, I tried to be as inconspicuous as possible and not cause any problems for anyone.

My mother was the tender, affectionate, cuddling one. I can't remember her hurting my feelings too much as I was growing up. She was a codependent, making sure everything got taken care of and that my father's needs were looked after. She was very controlling. In some ways I enjoyed her control, because it meant I wouldn't have to make any decisions. Whenever we'd go clothes shopping, she'd always tell me what I should wear. I really didn't learn how to make decisions on my own or how to develop my own personal tastes. My tastes were her tastes, and I didn't challenge that at all.

One of the biggest areas of confusion for me while I was growing up was my gender. For a number of years I didn't really know if I was a girl or a boy. I kind of felt like I was both. I was a tomboy who always hung around with the guys or played sports.

When I did play with my girlfriends, I usually had the boy-roles. I had two friends who loved to play house. They'd ask me to come over and I'd bring my "girl-type" toys with me. They'd always play the role of the mothers and wives; I'd play the husband. First they'd wait on me, feeding me breakfast and making sure my clothes looked all right to go off to work. Then off to work I'd go. That would be the boring part for me, because all I did was hang around while they played out their roles until I came home from work.

But the greatest thing about playing that game was the feeling of being waited on and having someone take care of my needs. In the role I was playing, my needs came first while other lives were focused on mine. That's what I believed a relationship was all about — taking care of someone else's every need.

In high school, I started to deal with my feelings of being attracted to women. I dated boys a few times, but preferred to spend my time playing women's sports and hanging around women.

I didn't act on those feelings until I was in my twenties and working full-time. I met a woman I felt sorry for. I wanted to take care of her. Then one night she told me she was attracted to me. It felt wonderful and flattering, that feeling of somebody wanting me. We started a relationship that lasted for four years.

But the relationship didn't turn out to be so wonderful. First, the role I played in that relationship was a continuation of me being the dumb one. She was supposedly the smart one and the one who made all the decisions. Second, she was very controlling of me like my mother had been. I guess I took on my father's role, for I'd do the heavy chores or be the one to take on the responsibility for seeing that things got done, like the cooking and the cleaning.

I felt I had to do an awful lot to keep the relationship together. I really didn't feel adequate or even equal to her. I believed her needs came first. When she wanted to build her dream house, I made that my dream house too and began the project with her.

The night before we were supposed to move into the house, she stayed out all night with a man. But I didn't walk out on her. We didn't even discuss that night and why she wanted to be with someone else. Instead, I still believed our relationship would work and we moved into our house. But she stayed out a lot. Essentially, I lived alone in the big, empty house. I spent a great deal of time trying to figure out what I had done to cause our relationship to end. I felt really embarrassed that I wasn't able to hold my "marriage" together. I felt like a failure. I stayed up many nights in that house, alone and crying in my pain.

I stayed away from relationships for two years after that because I thought I couldn't get one to work. I had grown up believing I should be in one relationship that would last for the rest of my life, and I believed I had failed. How could I possibly do any better than what I had done?

Then I sold my half of the dream house. A few weeks later, I started on my second relationship. I remember thinking to myself that I didn't really want to be involved with the woman, but I didn't want to hurt her feelings. So I stayed in that relationship for six years! She was an alcoholic who was starting recovery in A.A. I attended a few A.A. meetings with her, and some of the things that were said at the meetings made sense. I quit drinking then too, but only on my willpower and not through the help of the program.

I found myself taking care of my second lover financially and emotionally. I believed that was what I should do, but I was very unhappy inside. After six years, I imagined myself in love with another woman and broke up with my lover. I felt a lot of fear about being alone, but then I got involved in another.

I didn't realize it, but a pattern was starting to form in my relationships. I'd get involved because I'd believe "this one would be the one that would last." Then it wouldn't last. I'd feel okay outside of the relationships, then someone would come along who was attracted to me, and I'd fall into another relationship.

It was a cycle with no end.

What is now . . .
I became involved with women's spirituality and one day picked up a brochure from a center that offered courses and workshops. As I read through the pamphlet, I came across a list of fourteen questions. I started answering them — yes . . . yes . . . yes. At the end of the list there was a description of a four-week course dealing with Adult Children of Alcoholics. I signed up.

At first I was scared. Those sessions touched on many feelings that been silent within me for years. Many times after an evening at the center I would drive home very fast, not caring whether I hit a tree or not. Often I'd want to drink.

I remember one night in particular. That's when I got in touch with a lot of anger I felt toward my father. The course facilitators asked us to get in touch with a time when we were very angry as a child. We were supposed to punch a pillow to release that anger. At first I was like ice. I thought nothing could shake me and get me to feel that anger.

Then I had a sudden flashback about a time when I was in the third grade. I belonged to the Girl Scouts, and they were having a father-daughter dinner. My father went to my brother's functions all the time, so I believed my father would come with me. But he refused. I was crushed. Inside, however, I kept alive a small hope that he'd change his mind. Even on the night of the dinner, I still hoped he'd walk through the door and say with a smile on his face, "I've changed my mind. I'll take you. "

That never happened. I went to the dinner by myself and held back my tears the whole time. I was so hurt. I was in so much pain. I wanted to cry out, "Why couldn't you go?"

When that memory popped into my mind, I felt like running away and getting drunk. I wanted to smash my car into a tree. I wanted to do anything but feel that pain all over again.

By the end of the four-week course, I had made a commitment to the group that I would start going to A.A. and/or Adult Children of Alcoholics meetings. I started going to A.A. first, then attended my first ACOA meeting.

At that first meeting I listened and felt for the first time that people could really understand me. I think I even introduced myself during that meeting just to hear myself talk in that room with those people. It was incredible, all the things they were saying, and I was in tears most of that meeting and afterwards. I could relate to what people were saying and knew my feelings were understood.

As I kept going to the ACOA meetings, I met other people who were gay. In fact, there was a meeting one time where the topic was sexuality and many people introduced themselves as gay. But gay or straight, that night they all said things I could relate to about being in relationships. I learned it didn't matter what my sexuality was. What was most important was how I felt being an adult child.

I learned too that people — both gay and straight — had difficulty forming healthy relationships. Many, like me, drifted from relationship to relationship, hoping to start feeling better about themselves. They also had looked to a relationship to take away their feelings of worthlessness and abandonment.

What can be . . .

I've been in the program for a year and a half. It's given me a place to go to talk about many of the relationship issues with which I have difficulty. I'm in a relationship now, but I know I need to keep going to meetings because they bring some healthy attitudes and a positive energy into the relationship. I also need to keep being reminded to keep the focus on me in any relationship.

That's one of the gifts I've been given from the program, but there are many others. One has been knowing I'm not crazy and things will get better. Sometimes I still feel down, but I don't get as down as I used to. I always have a meeting I can go to. And the meetings always help me. I can walk into a meeting feeling really rotten and be given hugs and caring and concern from other people. I can then leave that meeting feeling a little more strength and hope than when I walked in.

Another gift has been a reconnection with my Higher Power and a renewed spirituality. I know today that something is there looking out for me. I know there are people in my life and I've been given challenges from which I need to grow. When I see any desperation today in my life, I can also see the answers are there for me too — when my Higher Power feels I'm ready to face them.

Finally, I have been given healthy tools to use in my relationships with people. In the past I had felt I always had to give someone 100 percent, whether that person was my lover, a friend, or even my boss.

Today, I work hard at maintaining a balance in my life so I'm not giving all of me away. I'm trying to feel okay even though I know I can't please everyone all the time.

The only person I need to please today is me. That relationship now takes priority over any other relationship in my life. *One day at a time*, I'm growing closer to realizing me.

ANGRY LOVE

Roy's Story — Age: 25

Love and time — those are the only two things in the world and all of life that cannot be bought, but only spent.

— Gary Jennings

There were two alcoholics in my family — my mother and my father. While my mother was kind and gentle and overly giving, my father was angry and verbally abusive. He is the one in my life with whom I have the most issues.

Growing up, all I ever really wanted from my parents and siblings was love. Yet it always seemed that the family was torn apart by angry, antagonistic behaviors fueled by alcohol. I felt miserable inside, but not only because of tensions and stresses. I also had my share of individual problems that made it difficult for me to cope. One of them was my obesity. Another was the fact that I, too, became an alcoholic.

When I left home a few years ago, I craved aloneness. Instead, I discovered loneliness. By joining the A.A. program, I came in touch with many of the issues I had inside and began to share them with other people. Still, there were issues related to growing up in an alcoholic home that I didn't discuss.

After a while I started attending Adult Children of Alcoholics meetings and learned I wasn't the only one who felt the way I did. I also discovered a difference between angry love and real love. And it is real love that I am finally beginning to feel for the first time in my life.

What once was . . .

I grew up in a family of eleven brothers and sisters. Some of them were from my father's first marriage and some from my mother's first marriage. We all weren't under the same roof at the same time. While I was growing up, I shared the house with two sisters and a brother. I was the second to the youngest.

Our household was always out of sync with my father's schedule. He worked evenings until eleven o'clock at night, and then his "after hours" began. He'd go to a bar after work, close it down, and then arrive home smashed at one or two in the morning. He was still raring to go, so he'd try to get the whole household up with him.

He was never quiet when he came home. I'd always hear him muttering and mumbling in the kitchen as he opened and closed the refrigerator door to grab more beer. Then he'd stumble into the living room, sink into a chair, and resume his drinking. While doing so, he'd make as much noise and commotion as he could.

I call his behavior on those work nights "getting things going." He was an angry man, and he would be damned if we were all going to sleep while he wanted us up and about. I'd lie in bed a long time, trying to ignore him by putting a pillow over my head. But then someone would yell out, "Shut up and let us get to sleep." That was like the sound of the bell to begin the first round of the nightly battle.

My father used the threat of physical violence and verbal abuse to battle each and every one of us. Because of the different parentage of each of the kids, he had a tremendous arsenal of anger, anguish, and blame to jab at all family members.

Once my father would get going, everyone would be drawn into the fighting ring — except me. I would sit at the top of the stairs and watch my sister nagging at him and my mother screaming at him. I'd hear the accusations and insinuations ring in my ears as each person tried to inflict as much damage as possible on the other. Everyone would be in the melee, throwing insults: "Your mother this . . ." and "Your father that . . ." I heard many things during those battles I wish I hadn't.

The rounds of fighting would stop when things were thrown or someone started to cry. Then I would leave my ringside seat to enter the arena in the role of referee. That wasn't easy because I really feared my father, but I knew someone had to take some action. I'd try to break up the fight so we could all get back to bed.

Although I was terribly frightened of my father, I was the only one who would really try to talk to him. I'd reason with him about putting away the alcohol and getting to bed, but he'd yell back at my face, "I'm gonna have another. There's nothin' to live for. I'm gonna drink!"

Sometimes I'd take his beer and dump it out, hoping that would stop him from drinking. But he'd threaten me with comments like, "Who do you think you are? Wanna fight? Huh, huh? Ya wanna?" I didn't want to fight with him. I never wanted to fight anybody. I just wanted all the anger and tension and drinking to stop. So I'd give up trying to get him to stop drinking. Instead, I'd sit up with him. Gradually he'd quiet down

82

as he sank into alcoholic oblivion. The house then settled back into its night's rest.

I'd think then about how I wanted to stop things, but I didn't know how. I felt like I never solved anything because there was no control over my father or his drinking.

My mother was a kind person who would give you the shirt off her back. But she too had a drinking problem. My father drank at night; my mother drank during the day at home. I could always tell when she had been drinking by the slur in her speech.

I can't remember if she drank every day. I do know when she got a job her drinking eased up a bit. But she still drank, and that really bothered me. I can recall asking her while she was drunk, "Ma, why do you have to drink?" She'd cry and say to me, "Roy, I just want to show him (my father) what an ass he looks like."

I hated my mother's drinking just as much as my father's. Inside, I felt a furnace burning hotter every time I saw one of them drunk. I wanted to ignore them, avoid them, run away from them, but I couldn't. I'd always end up being there for them, talking to them, and feeling responsible for making things better.

I found my own ways to cope while growing up. One way was by eating. I was very obese as a child. Because of that, I never fit in with any of the kids. They were cruel to me about my weight and the biting, vicious remarks they made hurt me a great deal. I wanted so badly to run fast like them and do all the things they could, but I was just too fat.

I remember I would come home from school and easily eat two small chickens. Or I'd down a whole box of cereal. I knew I definitely ate in quantities that weren't appropriate for a normal person, but I didn't know what to do to stop.

My mother didn't help the situation. She was used to feeding a large family, so she cooked for us as if there were eight people at home. I believe she thought she was doing a good thing for me by cooking foods I really liked, but I thought she was being cruel to me. I couldn't resist the foods she laid out before me. I felt helpless. All I could do was eat and eat and eat.

Another way I coped was by escaping into my own little dreamworld. My parents didn't seem to notice as much as my teachers did. The comments on the backs of my report cards were often "Roy is a good student in class. But he doesn't work to the best of his ability and he constantly daydreams."

I became an expert at watching television during the most chaotic times. My father hated television, but he hated it even more if someone else was watching TV and having a good time. He'd come into the living room when we were all enjoying a show such as The Wonderful World of Disney. He'd start nagging about how bad television was and his voice would roar, "Television is the worst thing ever made!" One by one, everyone would nibble on the bait until the whole room fell into the trap of an argument — all except me. I'd still watch television. I'd block out what was going on around me and retreat into my head.

A final way I learned to cope with the tension and turmoil at home was by drinking. When I had my first drink of alcohol, I drank myself blind and then came home to the usual family sparring battle. I walked upstairs, passed out on the bed, and slept right through it all. The alcohol helped numb my reaction to the battle, and I loved that feeling. I started to drink more and often.

As I grew older, I spent a lot of time with my father, despite my fear of him. I went with him on camping, hunting, or fishing trips for a couple of reasons. One was I felt good getting him out of the house and away from my mother and sisters. Knowing I might be making them feel better made me feel better.

The other reason was I loved being outdoors. I think my father did too, but those trips always seemed to be yet another excuse for drinking. My fun was usually ruined by his getting drunk and acting crazy. As the day wore on, I looked forward to the time when we'd go home and wouldn't have to be together anymore. On the drive home, I'd sit tensely in the car as his white-knuckled passenger, praying we'd arrive home safely.

When I was 21 or 22 years old, my parents separated. My mother and one of my sisters moved into an apartment. I stayed with my father. Living with him, I was no longer able to ignore his baiting. He didn't have anyone else to "get going" with when he came home from work except me. Like a fool, I fell into his trap every time by yelling, screaming, and arguing with him like he wanted.

Many times I felt like I wanted to hit him. But I'd always turn around and get a grip on myself. One night I lost that grip, however, and blew up and hit the refrigerator. I almost broke my hand.

Things were getting more and more out of control, and I knew I had to do something about it — fast.

What can be . . .

I knew I had to leave that unhealthy environment, but I felt guilty. Many times my father had threatened suicide, and I was afraid my leaving would trigger an attempt.

I was rapidly falling into a horrible emotional bottom. My drinking had gotten worse. It was so bad, people started to tell me that maybe I had a drinking problem. But I never believed them. All I had to do was look at my father to know who had a drinking problem. Then one night I hit bottom. I had come home from a skiing trip and decided to get help. I looked up the A.A. hotline number in the telephone book. My father was watching me and asked, "Who are you calling?" I didn't tell him at first, then I spit it out.

I attended an A.A. meeting the next night and kept going back. Little by little, A.A. was helping me get sober. It wasn't easy to stay sober because I had to come home every night to my father's drinking and angry behavior. I knew I had to get out of there, or I wasn't going to be able to work my program well at all.

I also knew that I had to get out on my own and learn what it was like to take care of myself. All my life, I had been cooked for and cleaned for. Even my father continued to make enormous meals for me and expect me to eat them. I wanted — and needed — to get away from him and start taking care of Roy.

I finally left home at 23 years old, lived with my sister for nine months, then bought my own house. I thought I'd learn how to be responsible if I had my own place. But instead of the house becoming my heaven, it turned into a haven. I used it as my "hiding place." I became afraid to live with anyone else.

I kept going to A.A. My attitudes began to change toward people around me, but not toward my family. They still tripped my triggers. So I started to attend Al-Anon meetings. In those meetings, I could identify with the feelings my parents probably had but not with how I felt growing up with their drinking. I still had the feeling that something wasn't right in my life, but I didn't know where to go with those feelings.

About a year after I had been in A.A., another recovering alcoholic told me about the Adult Children of Alcoholics meetings. I was really afraid to go to my first meeting alone because I thought Adult Children meetings were like therapy sessions. I dragged three other A.A. people with me. But when I heard someone read the list of fourteen identifying questions of an adult child, I wanted to know how I could join. That night, at my first meeting, I raised my hand and shared a little bit about how I felt.

I went home that night and cried because I wanted more, so much more, than that first meeting, and I wanted it all at once. That meeting had opened the door for me. I knew I wasn't alone anymore, and I wanted to have that feeling reinforced.

I went a little overboard with ACOA in the beginning because I ignored my A.A. My sobriety almost suffered because I became withdrawn and isolated. But I was reminded by others in the program that I was an alcoholic and had to put A.A. first to treat my disease.

When I found the balance that was right for me in A.A. and ACOA, I truly started to benefit from both programs. I began to grow in leaps and bounds.

What can be . . .

I've learned a great deal about Roy in the ACOA program. One of the most important things I've come face-to-face with has been my concern for others rather than myself. All my life, I worried that I'd never be compatible for somebody else in a relationship. Now I've learned that I need to look for others to be compatible with *me*. What a big step: learning how to put myself first instead of others.

I've also come in touch with how desperately I need to be loved. Growing up, all I ever wanted from my parents and siblings was to be loved. During our family arguments, one of my sisters would always threaten to run away. I would be devastated when she said that, because I wanted her never to leave. I recall crying and begging her not to leave the house. But I had never told her nor really shown her that I loved her. I didn't know how to because I had never learned what real love was all about — the hugging and caring and communicating. That kind of affection was shown to me at the ACOA meetings, and I couldn't seem to get enough of it in the beginning.

Today, I can tell my sister I love her. And I can show her, too, by giving her hugs. My father is a different story. He's gone to a couple of ACOA meetings with me. I've gone up to hug him a couple of times, but his acceptance of me is not there yet. That hurts me a lot.

The program has taught me, however, to be grateful for the small miracles as well as the big. So I am grateful today that he's going to these meetings on his own. I know it's a big step for him to try to understand and share in something that means a great deal to me.

I believe the greatest gifts of the program are the trust in people I now have and my ability to share with them who I really am. I've even started to trust myself.

I know my progress today is slower than I'd like it to be. I want everything *now* — the beautiful home, wonderful friends, warm family, and terrific relationships. But I need to slow myself down. For me to be happy with myself and other people, I need to keep my personal goals simple and my daily life uncluttered.

Someday, I want to be loved and want to love somebody in return. I know that day will happen because I have found so many answers in a wonderful program that's based upon real love.

MOTHER, DAUGHTER, DAUGHTER

Elena and Sheila's Story — Ages: 42 and 32

People are what they are because they have come out of what was.
                                                    — *Carl Sandburg*

Our father was the alcoholic, but our mother was the one who we both had issues with. She was a cruel, inconsistent, insensitive woman who made life miserable for us in different ways.

Surprisingly, even though our father had many close calls and hospitalizations because of his drinking, he didn't affect us as powerfully as our mother did. We saw our father as a weak but kind man who didn't have a mean bone in his body.

After leaving the house to venture out into the world as adults, we found ourselves affected by people, places, and things in similar ways. Our childhood memories began to play a part in our adult lives. Gradually, we started to share some of the feelings we'd been holding inside since our childhood. One of us, then the other, became involved in Adult Children of Alcoholics.

Today we're both involved in the ACOA program. We attend many meetings together and talk frequently about what it was like for each of us to grow up in the same alcoholic home. Although our growth in the program is painful at times, it's great to be able to have each other there for validation of our past and for support in the present.

Even though we grew up in the same alcoholic home, our stories are different. But our feelings are the same.

What once was . . . for Elena . . .

I was the oldest of six children. What I remember the most about my childhood is playing the role of mother to the rest of the children and co-spouse to my father.

My father worked days and my mother worked nights, the three to eleven shift. As soon as I'd come home from school, my mother would leave for work and I'd have to take care of the kids. I'd get supper for my father and my brothers and sisters, see that the dishes got done, get the kids ready for bed, then settle down to do my homework.

89

If I could draw a picture of what I looked like back then, I would show a little girl standing on a chair as she reached into the sink to do the family's dinner dishes. She was the one in charge of everything. The entire household rested on her shoulders while Ma was off at work.

I hated every minute of my "mother" role. I also hated my father's expectations that I do all the chores around the house and be there with supper waiting for him when he came home from work.

I was the superresponsible child who was treated by my parents as an adult. I hated the responsibility of being wife and mother, and I also hated being put in the middle between my mother and father. They rarely got along. One of the favorite tactics they used while fighting was to not communicate directly with each other. Instead, I was employed by them as a sort of switchboard operator who relayed their messages back and forth.

A typical message relay would go like this. My father would say to me, "Tell your mother this . . . " and I'd run to my mother to tell her what my father had said. My mother would reply, "Tell your father that . . ." and I'd go running back to him to tell him the message. Back and forth I'd go, hoping maybe they'd make up soon and everything would start to be good in the house.

I remember always feeling nervous and anxious inside. One of my habits as a child was to rub my hands together. I used to go up to my room, stand there, and just rub and rub my hands together. I guess it was my way of releasing the tension around the house. That tension was definitely a result of my mother's actions and reactions.

I could never seem to please my mother. I would clean the house from top to bottom, making everything gleam and shine. Then she'd come home from work, see a jacket lying on the couch, and start screaming about that. She never noticed what had been done, only what hadn't.

I called the times when my mother would rant and rave her "flip out" times. Those times were very scary and extremely stressful. I never knew when she'd start flipping out or what would cause it. During those times, she didn't care if God was in the house with the Pope. She would yell and scream in front of guests as well as family. After a while, I stopped bringing friends to the house. It was too embarrassing.

I was ashamed to have anyone see my mother when she was in a "flip out." I guess I felt if my mother didn't look good, then I didn't look good either. I wanted to look perfect, not only to my mother, but also to my friends. Friends were very important to me, because they were my way out of the tension and crazy behavior. So I didn't want to have anything happen that would ruin that.

I tried really hard to be good. I tried really hard to be perfect. I felt if I was the best I could be, things would get better. So I kept trying and trying. But nothing ever changed.

What once was . . . for Sheila . . .

I grew up ten years after Elena. By that time my parents really weren't talking to each other at all. A tense silence filled the house all the time. There was no love expressed or affection shown between my parents or toward us kids. I grew up feeling like I had been adopted because I just didn't feel loved at all.

My mother was a bitter, frustrated person who took her feelings out on her kids. I turned out to be one of her favorite targets. As a child I was very heavy and self-conscious of it. I also was a bed wetter. Those two problems made me feel isolated and lonely and extremely vulnerable. Those two areas were the ones my mother usually attacked.

I remember when I was nine or ten years old I was able to go away on a school trip with the band. I was really nervous about that because I was afraid I'd wet my bed and then everyone would find out about my problem. But my mother had "taken care" of that problem for me. She had told the chaperone ahead of time about my bed wetting. That night at the hotel, the chaperone said to me in front of all the other kids, "Now, Sheila, make sure you go to the bathroom before you go to bed." I was humiliated. I just wanted to go home.

But home was no better. When my mother came home from work after eleven o'clock, she'd wake me up so I could go to the bathroom. Sometimes that meant my bed would be dry in the morning, but oftentimes it wouldn't. There were times when my mother made me eat tons of bread — regardless of my weight problem — hoping the bread would soak up the liquids so I wouldn't wet my bed.

Most nights, however, I wet my bed. My mother would be furious with me, screaming loudly and waking up the whole house. Everyone knew then that Sheila had wet her bed. She'd make me change the sheets myself. Lots of times, to punish me, she made me wash and dry the soiled sheets and use them to make my clean bed. On those nights, I didn't get back to bed until two or three in the morning.

Many times Elena would come in and comfort me. Even though my parents never gave us hugs, the siblings would give each other a lot of love. So Elena would come in, hug me, and say to me, "What a nut Ma is." She helped me feel better.

Lots of times I didn't care how mother treated me. I had no problem defying her, even though that meant getting beat on. She'd rarely raise a hand to Elena because Elena tried to do everything right so Ma wouldn't get mad. But I didn't care about making Ma feel better. I just wanted her to stop making *me* feel so bad.

One day we were eating lunch at the table and my mother got mad at me and poured a bowl of soup on my head. I had to go back to school that day like that. Another time she was angry at me and started hitting me. I was crying and she didn't like that, so she kept hitting me to make me stop. After a while she had me on the floor, beating on me. One of my sisters screamed out, "Ma, you're going to kill her!" My mother replied, "Well, I want to kill her. She drives me crazy!"

I was different from Elena in that I didn't care whether I pleased Ma or made her happy. I didn't care. I didn't get as upset as Elena did about cleaning the house. Rather than get upset over the incomprehensible things my mother would do, I'd just let it roll off my shoulders. There was no pleasing that woman.

For example, for years every Friday afternoon after school three of us had to wash and wax the kitchen floor. It was a long, tiring procedure because we had to strip off the old wax and put on two coats of new wax.

But Ma would come in the door — rain, hail, sleet, or snow — with her boots all covered with grime. By this time we would have put a few hours into the backbreaking work. We'd yell out to her, "Ma! Ma! The floor's not dry yet!" But that didn't seem to matter to her. She'd look at us, stonefaced, then point to a corner of the floor and say, "You missed that corner."

I could hardly wait to get out of the house.

What is now . . . for Elena . . .

I left home as soon as I could and escaped into a convent. That didn't last for long, so I came home and went to work. But I was really unhappy. I met a man shortly after that who asked me to marry him one week after I met him. I don't know why, but I said yes. I guess I felt marrying him was the only way I could get out of the house.

Little did I know, however, that he was a carbon copy of the behavior I had grown up with. If I told him how I felt, for example, he'd stop talking to me. If I brought up an issue that concerned me, he would tell me I was crazy. I usually ended up apologizing to him in the end for things I said or felt because I started to believe maybe I was crazy. I started to accept blame for anything that happened in the house.

We had two children. Both children turned out to be chemically dependent — my son is an addict and my daughter an alcoholic. The marriage was going from bad to worse. Then communication ceased. I remembered at the time thinking back to my parents' marriage and saying to myself, "I'm not going to let this marriage get this bad. I'll leave before that happens."

After twelve years in the marriage, I left with my children.

The first thing I did was get help for my son, but it was recommended that I, too, needed treatment. I signed up for the week-long family treatment program, and my son entered his phase of treatment. What happened to me at the treatment center led me to Adult Children of Alcoholics.

In treatment I had to uncover my feelings as a child growing up in an alcoholic home. These feelings were buried under layers of thick protection that I formed in order to function in the world on my own. But once they did surface, I felt intense sadness and pain.

After that week was over, I was actually numb. My mouth was wide open with all the realizations that were uncovered about my past. I was then given my "prescription" for ongoing treatment — attend ACOA meetings.

I knew I had to fill that prescription in order to get better. My denial was lifting. I now had the courage to admit I was powerless and was ready for whatever the program had to offer, even though it was very painful in the beginning. In fact, things got a whole lot worse before they got better. When I came out of the treatment center I was on a high. I was feeling good that people were finally listening to me and understanding how difficult it was for me to grow up in an alcoholic home.

But when I got home I tried to do the whole program in thirteen days. I found out it didn't work that way. What I wanted was for the pain of the past to immediately disappear. So I'd attend meetings and go from one extreme to the next. One week I'd say, "Oh, I really identify with the speakers and what they had to say." But the next week I might feel differently. Those times I'd think to myself, "Come on, Elena, your life wasn't really all that bad. You don't need this program."

But then someone who had been in the program a while told me to listen to my feelings instead of trying to identify with the circumstances of the stories I was hearing at meetings. Once I did that, my growth really began to blossom.

What is now . . . for Sheila . . .

When I graduated from high school, I had lost about a hundred pounds. I went from an obese, lonely girl who stayed in every night of the week for four years to a nice-figured woman going out every night of the week. I loved it.

I got a job, and a man at work asked me out. Within two months, we left for California together. I was so swept away with him. He was the first person who ever told me he loved me. I didn't know what to do with that, but I also knew I didn't want him to go away.

We came back from California and I ended up marrying him. I wasn't in love with him. I didn't even really like him that much. I don't think I even knew how to be honest with him. But I guess I thought marriage to him would be a way for me to get out of the house.

Marriage was far from blissful. When he got angry — which was often — he behaved just like my mother had by throwing temper tantrums. When I looked into his rage-crazed eyes, I saw my mother's eyes when she was on her rampages.

At first my husband was the sole breadwinner, but then I got a well-paying job. I started to feel good about myself. He clearly didn't like that at all. Although I could feel strong and confident when I wasn't with him, with him I was like a little girl. He still had all the control. His rule was final.

I stayed in close contact with Elena throughout her family treatment and divorce. We talked frequently. I started to learn a lot from her and saw her growing in a way I wanted to grow. She attended adult children's meetings regularly and told me things like, "I have to remember to take things one day at a time," or "I have to stop thinking of other people and start thinking of myself." The things she was telling me were starting to sink in. I really liked what she had to say.

But my communication with my other sisters wasn't as good as with Elena. My husband and I had arranged a trip to Hawaii with two sisters. We hadn't been in the air for more than two hours when I said something and one of them snapped back at me, "What are you? Getting uppity like Elena?"

For the rest of the trip, they snubbed my husband and me. We were never included on anything they did around the island. When I got home, Elena and I eventually talked about my trip and I learned for the first time what Elena felt like growing up in our house. I learned how much those sisters didn't like her because our mother made her into an authority, a mother figure.

That trip to Hawaii helped me understand my sister better. It also made me listen more closely to things Elena was telling me about the ACOA program. I remember one night she brought me the list of fourteen questions about whether one is an adult child. I went into my bedroom after she left, closed the door to the room, and sat huddled up as I read the list. With every question, I started to wonder who had been looking in my windows or taping me. It was as if someone had written those fourteen questions specifically for me!

I wasn't ready for the program until my father had another of his bad drinking bouts. They had happened before, and I had always been there to clean him up, take care of him, or rush him off to the hospital. This time was no different. I walked into a house reeking of urine, soiled by blood, and littered with trash and human feces.

My father was slumped in the corner of the couch. I took one look at him and said to myself, "I'm sick of taking care of him." I turned around and walked out the door. That night he was hospitalized. My sister, who was an R.N., called and told me, "You'd better come. This is it. I think he's going to die." I'd heard that so many times before, and he had never died. This time I wanted to go into that hospital and scream at him, "If you want to die, then stop putting us through this!"

I had very little feelings left for my father. He survived that bout, then had another in January of 1985. My sister called and told me, "You've got to come. You're the only one he'll listen to." I said no, without even thinking twice.

That night, I called Elena. I told her I couldn't believe what I had just said to our sister and added, "I think I'd better start going to meetings with you."

What can be . . . for Elena . . .

As I continued to go to meetings, things got better. I did a lot of reading about the disease of alcoholism and adult children's issues. I even began to feel some anger, which is an emotion I had never allowed myself to feel during my life.

I learned, through the treatment center and ACOA, that I had grown up with crazy behavior and had married into the crazy behavior of three active chemically dependent people — my husband, my son, and my daughter. With all that craziness around me, I found out I didn't get crazy all by myself. I got crazy for a reason.

Today I've been in the program two years. For the first time, I have my own life. I have choices I never thought I had before. I have hope for the present and future and a faith that ACOA was a gift to me from God. Perhaps one of the greatest gifts of the program has been in my relationship with Sheila. She's really the only family I feel I have now. She and I can talk about real issues — feelings — like we never could before.

It's a real benefit to my growth to have my sister in the program with me. She and I can go to the same meetings and get two totally different things out of it. It's great to be able to listen to her point of view. She helps me see myself and tells me to ease up on myself if I'm being too hard on me.

Because of ACOA, I've been given my sister Sheila. When I was growing up, I was made to feel like I was the mother of the family. Even though I had siblings, I never knew what it was like to have them. Now I know what it's like to have a sister. For that I am forever grateful.

What can be . . . for Sheila . . .

When I first got into the program, the initial meetings were kind of heavy and scary to me. I had stuffed my feelings so deep I couldn't relate when people talked about their feelings. I remember hearing people share and thinking to myself, "Wow! I'm glad I don't feel that way." I don't think I knew how to feel. I didn't even know what sad was, and I couldn't remember the last time I had cried or felt happy.

Then I started to change. I got the courage to stand up to my husband and refused to be treated by him the way he had treated me. Today that marriage is over.

I've been in the program a year and four months. There are so many things I hope for myself in the future, and I know my dreams can be realized. I want to take life lighter. I don't want to be so serious about things. I want to be spontaneous, relax, and let my guard down a little. I am more relaxed than I've ever been in my life because of ACOA, and each day it gets a little easier.

Having my sister in the program helps. Since she's had more time and experience, I've come to use her as my sponsor. We share our deepest, darkest fears. With Elena, I don't hold anything back. I know she'll understand what I'm saying and accept me for who I am.

In a way I feel like we're in a training program for something. What, I don't know. But I do know I like the way I'm going. As long as she's only a phone call away, I'm ready for anything the program can give me.

WHERE DO I BELONG?

Amy's Story — Age: 32

A child is often an innocent by-product.

— *Anonymous*

I used to wonder what things would be like if Margery had never been an alcoholic. Sometimes I'd imagine the type of family we would've been. My Dad once told me things could've been just fine if she hadn't drunk. He said there was a lot of love and that we would've been very happy together as a family.

To this day I don't believe I know what a family is, yet I yearn for it. I yearn for the sense of belonging, the sense of connection, the sense of common purpose from a shared name and a shared roof. Growing up, I never knew where I belonged or who I belonged to, and I brought this sense of loss and confusion into my adult life.

I'm grateful I wasn't brought up in an actively alcoholic home. Yet even though the bottle and the drinker left while I was very young, their ghosts remained. During my impressionable growth years, those around me and the circumstances I was brought into were directly affected by the disease of alcoholism.

What once was . . .

I was put up for adoption at birth and almost immediately placed under foster parent care. This first home was a temporary one until I could be permanently placed. Soon after, Margery and my dad adopted me.

Things hadn't been easy for them up to that point because Margery couldn't conceive. She had started drinking heavily, which my Dad thought was due to her childlessness. They decided to adopt. After the usual interviews, they were approved and waited impatiently for the next available matching baby. They were never happier than when they were able to adopt me. With me, they had hope that all would be well with their marriage and with Margery's drinking.

But she didn't stop drinking when I came to live with them. She got up every morning and made my dad breakfast before he left for work, but after he left her, drinking would start. My dad would sit at his office and worry about me. When he'd arrive home, Margery would usually be drunk.

Apparently she tried A.A. — many times. But she couldn't seem to completely put away the bottle. My father wasn't the only one who noticed her problem. A next-door neighbor sometimes saw her stagger to the car with me and then drive off. Finally, the neighbor could stay quiet no longer and called the state authorities. I was placed in a temporary home until Margery could work out her drinking issue. I was two years old.

This second foster home was nice. I loved my foster mother; I called her "Mom." But I didn't pay much attention to my foster father. I still knew I had a "real" father, because my dad would pick me up every weekend and take me to do things with him. Those weekends were wonderful for me, but I'd bawl my eyes out when he drove me back to the foster home on Sunday night. I think I lived to see my dad. I loved him dearly and was very attached to him.

While I was in the foster home, my dad and Margery were divorced. My father gained custody of me. I don't think I ever saw Margery again; for all I knew, Margery no longer existed. Now it was just my dad and me. I was six years old.

He hired a housekeeper to take care of me. I was a spoiled brat. I had the housekeeper waiting on me hand and foot. If I wanted a full-course spaghetti dinner in front of the television, I got it. If I wanted six chocolate floats for lunch, my wish was her command. I also had my dad wrapped around my little finger. He was filled with guilt over his failed marriage and motherless child and was only too ready to comply with my wishes.

Shortly after my dad and I had been living together, he began to date a woman. I didn't like her very much. Once he and I went over to her small studio apartment for dinner. I took one look at the food in the pot and declared, "I don't like it. I don't want to eat it." I could hardly wait until that evening was over and my dad and I were back home. But that wasn't the last time I saw her. She became my dad's new wife, and then everything in my life changed. For one thing, my dad wasn't at my beck and call anymore, nor was this new woman. In fact, she wanted to be around my dad so much that he and I rarely got to spend time together. This wasn't what I had in mind for a family.

She later became pregnant, but lost the baby and nearly died herself. As a result, she could never have children. She and I were just beginning to form a very cautious and slowly developing relationship, but the loss of her baby put all that on hold. Her disappointment was so devastating that our relationship was in jeopardy. We immediately began an angry battle that extended all the way into my college years.

I was the happiest during two periods of my life. The first was any time at all that I spent with my dad. The second was every summer that I went away to summer camp. I loved being away from home, even though I missed my dad a lot. But I didn't miss my new mother at all and hated the way she tried to take Dad away from me. For as long as I was away from home, I was able to live without the tension and anxiety.

The thing I liked most about summer camp was the feeling that I belonged. Every cabin had twelve to fifteen girls in it, along with two counselors. I loved the counselors and thought of them as my mothers. It was great having two mothers and feeling like I lived with all my sisters under the same roof. My fantasy was that I could stay year-round at this camp with the counselors and the campers and that we'd all take meals together and play together. It was absolutely idyllic for me there.

The counselors seemed to like me too. Perhaps they saw an aching need in me — a desperation to be loved and to belong. When I learned that doing well in my activities meant more approval and attention from them, I strived to excel in everything. Every two weeks, the counselors would give out awards in each activity to outstanding campers. I tried to get more than everybody else and was furiously jealous when anyone got more than I.

At the end of the summer, I returned home to live as an only child in middle-class luxury. I had a bedroom and a sitting room to myself, along with a stereo, radio, and color television. I felt so lost and alone in those rooms. It was as if I were living in my own house, and not in a home shared by people in a family.

My parents and I rarely did things together except for the necessary clothes shopping times and visiting family or family friends. I remember feeling very insecure around the newfound extended family we gained after my mother joined my dad and me. I felt I didn't belong at all on my mother's side of the family, and I refused to get close to anyone.

I really did like my new cousins, who were younger than I. I felt at times like an older sister to them, but that really didn't extend beyond the social gatherings we had. I would always feel like I didn't belong — no matter where I was — unless my dad and I were together.

There were times that I enjoyed going to parties with my parents. Those were usually the only times my mother would drink. She wasn't an alcoholic, but drinking changed her personality. Normally she was a quiet, unemotional woman who was very cold toward me. But during those social drinking occasions she would become a woman who was a pleasure to be with. She would be happy and free and sometimes laugh out loud. Even though these times were short, I loved them because she would be friendly to me. During those times, it almost seemed like we could get along as mother and daughter.

I think more than anything else in the world I wanted my mother, my dad, and me to get along. I desperately wanted to feel like I belonged in a family, yet I hated what was in ours. I'd visit friends and wish I could have what they had. Everyone seemed to do things together and laugh and help each other out and share. I felt totally abandoned in my family. I felt like my parents were together, but that I didn't belong to either one of them.

When I got to junior high school, I was miserable. My mother and I started having angry, screaming battles. I began to tell my dad how much I disliked this woman and how much she was breaking us apart. I wanted him to divorce her and go back to the time when he and I could be alone. Then I felt I'd be happy.

My dad was a codependent who tried to please everyone and yet not get involved. If I wanted to spend time with him, I'd beg him and throw tantrums until he did. Then when he'd spend time with me, my mother would get angry and jealous and make up excuses for him to be with her or for me to be off doing something else. My mother and I began a push-pull, tug-of-war with my dad while we tried to hurt each other as much as possible.

In high school I continued to feel absolutely miserable. I didn't seem to fit in anywhere. I was in the "smart" track, but that was about the only identification I had. I didn't do many extracurricular activities, and the ones I did participate in weren't the popular ones. I was an overweight, depressed, acne-faced youngster who hated herself.

The approval-seeking games I'd learned at summer camp weren't as effective at home. I learned to associate good grades with money. If I got an A, my dad gave me a dollar. If I got on the honor roll, I got congratulations. But if I had a basketball game to play in or a debate tournament to go to, neither parent would be available to watch or to give me a ride home.

One night, while watching television, I took ten Midol pills. I felt such hopelessness in my family and such hatred for myself that I wanted to die. But instead of dying, I spent a sleepless and miserable night being very sick. The next morning, I told my parents I had taken the pills. They made sure I was physically okay, but that was the end of any attention paid to this first suicide attempt.

It wasn't until I got to college that I began to feel a sense of self. Away from home, I felt more relaxed and peaceful. I was fascinated by all the people around me and their different lives. I loved working hard in my studies and choosing courses. My grades were excellent, and I became fairly popular with other students and the professors.

During the summers I returned to summer camp as a counselor. I loved being a counselor because the campers looked up to me and worshiped me. During those times, I learned what it felt like to be loved and adored for who I was. I wanted summer camp and college to go on forever, but those four years flew by.

After graduation, my life was extremely stressful and chaotic. Suddenly I was out on my own, and I hated it. Being an unmarried person near a big city was frightening and lonely. Making friends was a slow process. Mostly I focused on relationships and yearned for a long-term, let's-settle-down relationship. I wanted to be taken care of and to take care of. I wanted to form my own family.

But none of my relationships seemed to last very long. I was a very clutching, obsessive person who was ready to put down my life for the person I loved. I rearranged schedules and bent over backwards to be with my lover. After a while, the relationship would end because I would smother the other person.

After yet another short-term relationship, I felt helpless, hopeless, and totally unloved. I tried to kill myself by swallowing 80 sleeping pills. Yet even when I was taking the pills I knew there was a big part of me that didn't want to die, that didn't want to give up the hope of someday being all right.

In my late twenties, I formed a relationship with a drug-addicted person. This wasn't the first time I had been in a relationship with an alcoholic or user, yet this was the first time I was also seeing a therapist.

It was recommended I start attending Al-Anon. After the relationship broke up, my therapist recommended a family treatment program and membership in Adult Children of Alcoholics.

Although I never viewed Margery's alcoholism as a problem in my life, I soon learned I had been directly affected by her drinking. Even though Margery left when I was two years old, her disease affected my dad, his relationship with me and his second wife, and my relationship with anyone. Margery's drinking left scars on us all.

What is now . . .

The first time I walked into an Al-Anon meeting, I listened but couldn't relate to people talking about drunken spouses or addicted children. But the first time I walked into an Adult Children of Alcoholics meeting, I knew I belonged. I knew that every person in that room understood the pain, the confusion, the anxieties, and the sadness I had felt all my life.

At the meetings I attended, fourteen questions were read at the start of the meeting. These questions were supposed to help you figure out if you needed the ACOA program. I answered yes to almost all of the fourteen questions, which covered issues from anger to self-esteem.

All my life, I had only felt anger and resentment at how my life turned out. I expected pity and affection from those who heard about my terrible childhood. "What a horror story," I wanted everyone to say. "How could you have survived? You are such a nice, nice person!"

I wanted other people to tell me I was a good, nice person because I certainly didn't believe I was. Yet even when people would compliment me or say how much they cared for me, I wouldn't believe them. I would believe instead that they were only saying those things to me because they wanted something.

ACOA gave me a chance to look at me in a way I never had before. Yet it didn't force me to do this, nor did any particular person. I merely kept going to meetings, listening to people talk, and sharing my own feelings. Little by little, I began to realize who I was. I began to identify areas that needed work in my personality, and I learned how to recognize the good qualities I had and could develop.

When I first came into the program, I was terribly angry at my mother, my dad, Margery, and at all the lovers that had ever left me. I was bitter about the abandonments in my life and held a grudge for each and every one of them. I believed things would have been fine if they hadn't worked out the way they did.

Slowly I began to look at the reasons for everything turning out the way it did. Gradually I learned to forgive my dad for his inability to make the family "all better. " I forgave my mother for her bitterness about her inability to have children. I forgave Margery for her inability to put down the bottle. I even forgave myself for my inability to accept people for who they were.

But I could only acquire this forgiveness with the development of a belief in a Power greater than myself. All my life I had rejected God and religion. I used to think it was hypocritical for my mother, father, and me to sit in a church pew and pray together like we were a family. I saw nothing redeeming or reassuring in the worship of God.

But the program spoke to me gently about a Higher Power, not necessarily God. I learned I could accept the existence of a greater force outside of me if I chose to and could ask this force for help and guidance.

I began to take the Steps of the program very seriously. I read literature and attended Step meetings to broaden my knowledge of their meaning. I used the gifts of these Steps in all areas of my life, and learned how to let go and let other people work on their issues while I worked on mine.

The program gave me strength to make my own decisions without feeling alone. Soon after I entered the ACOA Program, I started to make friends and stopped focusing on meeting someone to settle down with forever and ever.

In ACOA, I found the family I'd always wanted.

What can be . . .

About six months ago, I got up the courage to search for my birthmother. I found her and have met with her a few times. Her life has been touched by alcoholism too. Her first husband was an active drinker and there is some of the disease on her side of the family.

I don't know all the reasons I searched for her, but I think one relates to my forgiveness of the circumstances of my life. I know I held resentments against her for giving me up for adoption. For years, that initial abandonment always made me feel like I was born to be unloved and alone.

But she opened her arms and her family to me. Through finding her, I have gained a stepfather, two half sisters, and a half brother. To say that I've easily accepted this gain in one gulp would be a lie. Today I have difficulty becoming close to her and to many people, particularly in a family situation. But I have hope for easing many of the fears I have about becoming close to people I'm afraid I might lose.

Through my growth in the program, I have also gained an improved relationship with my mother and dad. Though we're far from being "The Brady Bunch, " I am now more ready to let them give me the love they are able to give — not necessarily the love I want them to give. I know if I want to talk to them or see them, I can ask. I'm not so afraid anymore to take risks of intimacy with them or with the family. In fact, I am starting to spend more time with my cousins outside of the family social gatherings, and that feels very good.

The only regret I have today is that I was unable to talk directly to Margery when I entered the program. She died of her disease when I was in my mid-twenties. At the time, her death had little meaning to me because I had pretty much forgotten about her ever being involved in my life. But as I grew in the program, I became more aware of the feelings I had toward her and how much I missed her. But I was able to make amends with her and forgive her for her past. My Higher Power helped me do that, and I finally put my feelings to rest.

In family treatment I learned the disease of alcoholism is threefold: mental, spiritual, and physical. For years, the disease certainly affected me in those areas.

Recovery in the program is also threefold. Today I have a spiritual belief, an improved physical appearance and attitude about my looks, and a positive mental attitude about my life and myself. Tomorrow holds for me a strengthening in all these areas. Today, and tomorrow, I belong wherever my life leads me.

THERE'S NO PLACE CALLED HOME

Stephen's Story — Age: 41

Fifty years ago parents were apt to have a lot of kids. Nowadays kids are apt to have a lot of parents.

— *Ernest D. Lawson*

My mother was an alcoholic whose disease rendered her totally incapable of caring for her five children. My brothers and sister, who were significantly older than I, assumed the roles of father and mother in order to take care of me.

When I was seven years old, my parents divorced. I stayed with my father until a violent argument drove me from that house into my aunt and uncle's. I stayed there for a short time, then was relocated to a new foster home. That home broke up in violence, too, so I landed back with my father and his new wife.

I spent most of my life crying out for nurturing and receiving none. So I learned the best methods to escape the pain. The only dream I had for myself was to be married and raise a family.

I married an alcoholic who confronted her own disease long before I acknowledged that my mother's alcoholism had affected me. When I finally did confront my past, a whole realm of feelings opened up before me. I started going to Adult Children of Alcoholics meetings to deal with my feelings.

Today I have found in ACOA the two things I desired all my life — security and affection. I have found my home today — with others who have shared a childhood taken away by alcoholism.

What once was . . .

My mother was an alcoholic who was generally incapacitated most of the time. Some of my earliest memories of her drinking were when I was five or six years old, in my preschool years. We would leave the house at midday, when my brothers and sister were in school. We'd drive to a barroom and stay there until the afternoon.

I remember the stench of those places and how dark they were. I always felt a little uncomfortable and fearful. I never knew what would happen there, and the atmosphere seemed mysterious and sinister. My mother was one of the few women in the place. She'd park me on a hard, wooden seat and buy me orange pop. That happened almost every weekday afternoon until I was old enough to go to school.

If my mother wasn't in the barroom drinking, she'd be locked in her bedroom or slumped on the couch. But the worst would happen when my father came home from work. When he'd find my mother drunk, he would become loud, abusive, verbal, and vulgar. And he'd beat her up.

My brothers and sister would try to get into the middle of the fights, but they'd only end up bruised and battered themselves. They did many things to try to help, such as throwing the booze down the drain and pleading for the drinking to stop.

I had a lot of fear during those times. I would hide and remain as insignificant as possible. There was a big, dark green chair that sat across the corner in the living room, and that's where I'd hide from my father's rampages and his beatings of my mother and siblings.

My father was so preoccupied with my mother, work, and his struggle to get an education in night school that he had little time to be a father to me. My older brothers, who were ten to fourteen years older than I, assumed the role of father. They took me to ball games and did things with me that made me feel special. My sister, who was seven years older than I, fulfilled the role of mother. She cooked and cleaned for me and made sure I took my baths. When she shared my caretaking with my brothers, I don't think I was too much of a strain to her.

My brothers enlisted and went to Korea as soon as they came of age. That was their escape from the house. The youngest of my brothers was so desperate to get out of the house that he was on his way to Parris Island as my family prepared to celebrate his birthday. My brother never showed up for the party.

When my last brother enlisted, my father left my care entirely in my sister's hands. While she became the most significant woman in my life, I was becoming a source of resentment for her. She was very unhappy about having to take care of me because she couldn't have a life of her own. She couldn't join Girl Scouts, socialize with girlfriends, or do any of the things that other girls her age would normally do. I felt guilty about her anger and resentments, but I couldn't do anything to change things.

My sister, however, took things in her own hands after a while. A short time after my father divorced my mother, my sister escaped by becoming involved with a soldier. She was fifteen or sixteen years old. My father was furious with her involvement and tried to get her to stop seeing the man. She wouldn't.

Then my father came home late one night and found the soldier in her bedroom. Even though they were only talking, my father hit the roof. He grabbed a baseball bat and started to hit them. I remember waking up that night to people screaming and running around the house. I watched from my bed, horrified. My father chased my sister and her boyfriend around my bedroom while he wielded the bat and shouted vulgar accusations at them. Blood was flying everywhere. All I could do was huddle under the covers and remain as invisible as possible.

Later that night, my sister disappeared. My father took off after her, leaving me alone in the house. He found her hours later and brought her home. The next day, she was being shipped off and so was I. She helped me pack my bags; then I left to live with my aunt and uncle for a while.

I was taken to a totally different neighborhood, away from all my friends, when I was nine years old. I was miserable. I hated being away from home, but mostly I hated being away from my old neighborhood and the people I had known. I had a best friend whom I was really attached to. In fact, people used to say he and I were like twins. But I couldn't see him anymore.

I felt unwanted in my aunt's home. She had two boys of her own and an alcoholic husband. She had her hands full, and I felt in the way most of the time. So I employed a method I had used quite successfully at home whenever things got too hot in the house — escape!

When I had been living at home, I had used the woods behind the house as a refuge from the anger, violence, and confusion. I had a secret place there and would hide or play by myself or with my friends. We'd have a great time playing John Wayne and GI Joe because the Korean War was on. I was really popular with the boys — sort of a folk hero — because my brothers were in the war and they'd give me their old stripes and medals. Whenever I was out in the woods, I felt on top of the world.

But in my new environment in the city with my aunt and uncle, there were no woods in which to disappear. So I found a new escape — the library. I'd spend hours there reading, or I'd check out books and take them to the back porch of my aunt's third floor apartment in the triple decker. If I couldn't successfully escape on that porch, I'd find any place where I could be alone and out of the way — a tool shed or even in the grapevines that grew in the garden.

I stayed at my aunt's for a few months; then my father found a foster home for me through the Catholic Charitable Bureau. Once again, I was off to a new environment.

I stayed in the new home for about a year and a half. Once again, I was in a new neighborhood with new people around me. This time, my escape became school. I became class president, worked hard for good marks, and became very attached to my classmates and to school in general.

Alcoholism still followed me into the new foster home. The man, whom I called my uncle, was an alcoholic. The woman, whom I called Mother, worked hard to take care of her husband and the other foster children in her home. In the short time I was there, I saw ten or eleven boys go through the doors. For most of the time, I had two older "brothers" there.

But that house broke up in violence when the oldest boy was caught stealing. After a big argument, the foster home was disbanded, and we were sent packing. I was scheduled to move back to my father's house three months from that time, but I had to go back home earlier.

My father had married a woman who was much older than he. She was so old she could have been my grandmother. Right away we had problems, partly because of the age difference and partly because she too was an alcoholic.

We battled constantly. One time I ran away and spent seven days in the woods alone. I had five dollars in my pocket and a .22 rifle. I bought beans and canned stuff to live on and refused to go home. I slept out in the open and took care of my needs.

My father used to brag about that time as if I were to be admired for what I had done. But I did that week-long escape to survive. I was hurting very badly inside. I was sick of moving around from house to house. I hated living alone with my father and stepmother. I missed my brothers and sister and couldn't understand why they had gone away and left me on my own.

I was desperate for love and affection. I don't recall ever getting a hug from anyone in my immediate family. Until that time, my father had never expressed caring toward me or told me he loved me.

I knew of only one way out of that existence.

What can be . . .

I had had one strong desire ever since I was five or six years old. That desire was to be married and raise a family. I didn't care about any career goals or material things. I just wanted to be married and have children.

As soon as I graduated from high school, I left home. Within three years, I was married. But my dream-come-true didn't come true. Marriage didn't solve all my problems or ease the pain I felt. Marriage was difficult for me. I had never learned to deal with someone else in a give-and-take situation. Because I had always been a survivor and looked out for myself, I didn't know how to stay put in the relationship when things needed to be discussed or worked out. The minute things started to get hot, I headed for the mountains or the seacoast. I didn't care where I went, just so long as I was away from the problems or disagreements.

I brought all my issues of abandonment and a history of foster homes into my marriage. Because of that, as desperate as I was for affection, I was always afraid it wouldn't work out. If things were going well, I waited for the other shoe to drop. If things were going badly, I was petrified I would be left.

I didn't know how to be happy in the marriage. I knew how to escape and find a certain amount of serenity and happiness for myself on my own, but I didn't know how to achieve that with someone else. Even though I was a very sensitive and caring person with human beings, any sort of closeness or intimate feelings expressed by my wife scared me.

I was so focused on myself in the marriage that I didn't notice my wife had a drinking problem. She started attending A.A. meetings, but I was reluctant to support her in the program because I didn't really believe she had a problem. After a short time, she strongly suggested I try Al-Anon. I went a few times — even had a sponsor — but I was kidding everyone — including myself. I believed I was going for my wife. At the time, I didn't think I had any problems as a result of her drinking . . . or anyone's.

Gradually, our marriage started deteriorating because she was growing and I wasn't. I was afraid to see our marriage failing. I found a therapist who reinforced my Al-Anon experience and recommended I check into a family treatment center.

I went to the center with my wife, but I was still kidding myself. I continued to believe I was going for her problem. Right after we got home from the center, we were on a pink cloud. Things couldn't have been better in our marriage, but that didn't last long. Things got bad again. I moved out for five months, then we got back together for a short time. Then we finally did separate.

That's when I started to hear the phrase, "adult child of an alcoholic" more and more. I started to listen because I was discovering that a great deal of my issues weren't being dealt with in the typical Al-Anon meeting. I started to attend Adult Children of Alcoholics meetings.

I had identified with many of the issues expressed at Al-Anon meetings, but felt a greater identity at ACOA meetings. The people seemed to be just like me. They all had a similar background with alcoholic parents. And they all talked about feelings I had too. Now, those feelings were ready to come out.

I learned I really had to get to work on myself and my particular issues, or I was never going to get better.

What can be . . .

One of the questions that had dogged me all my life was: How do I deal one-on-one in a relationship? I knew of only a few ways to cope with the intensity of person-to-person communication: escapism, martyrdom, and guilt trips. None of them were healthy answers or had good results.

But in ACOA meetings, I started to get some answers to that question. I started to confront my negative behaviors and listened to how others had dealt with questions similar to mine.

Today I desperately want to learn and change, and ACOA is helping me in many ways. I am coming in touch with new emotions. Prior to the program, I had been accustomed to feeling either anger or depression — nothing else. As I attended meetings, I started to feel feelings I had never felt before or been able to identify. Recently I felt sad, and I was kind of glad to feel that emotion. The next day, I felt happy. I was wearing a smile and even kidding around with people. Though those two times may not seem like much, for me they are milestones. If I can have two days of feeling happy or feeling sad, I know I can have more days of those honest feelings.

Perhaps the greatest gift of the program has been giving me to me. My wife accused me of running away from her, and my kids accused me of running away from them, but the bottom line was that I was running away from me.

ACOA has taught me that escape isn't the answer in forming relationships with people. When I wanted to escape before, I was always reacting to what was going on around me. Through the program, I've learned to not react in intense situations, but to act. I can use patience. I can bite my tongue, nail my feet to the floor, and think. I don't need to run away anymore, because that won't solve anything.

I wish the world could function like the program. There's no discrimination, no bias, no financial requirements. On any given night, two people from opposite sides of the spectrum can share the same feelings and understand what the other is talking about.

That's what I gain the most strength from in the program — the different people. It's through them that I've begun to satisfy two basic needs I've had all my life — security and affection. I knew nothing of either in growing up, but I get both from the program. I can attend a meeting and know that someone cares enough about me to ask how I am and what I'm doing. We can hug and I can know I belong.

There are very few places in my life where I've felt I've belonged. ACOA is one of them.

EVERYBODY WANTED MY PARENTS

Pam's Story — Age: 41

Parents are the bones on which children cut their teeth.

— *Peter Ustinov*

We looked like a family that should be starring in their own television series. We were regarded by the people in our small, southern town as the way a true southern family should look.

My parents maintained an air of sophistication in everything they did — from their mannerisms and interaction with people right down to their drinking. While I was growing up, drinking was a social endeavor of great pomp and circumstance, but it did not pose a problem in my upbringing.

Then, when I was 21 years old, I returned home from college to find Mother drinking heavily and getting visibly drunk. Suddenly the world I had known was shattered. Mother left Father, took up with an old flame, and continued to drink. I couldn't see alcohol was her problem because I, too, was drinking heavily. But when I reached my bottom, I could see alcohol was also Mother's problem.

After I joined A.A., I started attending Adult Children of Alcoholics meetings with my lover. After a few meetings, I started to identify with the feelings as if I, too, had grown up in the alcoholic home. Mother's late-blooming drinking caused me pain, but I also realized my childhood had been painful because Mother had tried to mold me into her own image.

Throughout my childhood, I learned how to look good on the outside. ACOA taught me how to feel good on the inside.

What once was . . .

I had the parents everyone else wanted. Daddy was from New York and Mother was the typical southern belle. They had met in New York City when Mother was assistant to the founder of a well-known modeling agency. Daddy was a man-about-town who worked in the theater and did some modeling himself.

They came back to our small, southern town and were known as the most handsome and most glamorous couple around. Daddy was the tall, dashing, quiet type, kind of a Gregory Peck or James Mason. He even looked like a famous Hollywood actor. Mother was petite and a dynamo. She had studied dance and was the outgoing, gregarious, social butterfly. Mother was the most popular person in town. She was a blend of Scarlett O'Hara and Doris Day. People remarked that she had the best personality around, and our house was always full of people.

Mother had a great deal of influence in our small town. She had a way of taking the most outlandish, out-of-the-ordinary people and making them acceptable to the conservatives around her. She used her influence to help the only homosexual in town establish a ballet school. He had come from New York City, owned dozens of poodles, and had purchased one of the oldest, most conservative homes in town and painted it purple. If that wasn't enough to stir up the town's citizens, he also boldly redecorated the interior of the home. But with Mother's help, his ballet school quickly became famous, and he became one of the wealthiest ballet teachers in the state.

Daddy and Mother's drinking was very sophisticated, done in *New Yorker* style. Daddy would mix their nightly martinis in a crystal pitcher with a silver top. They would have one or two, almost as a daily ritual.

Growing up, I saw drinking as very idealized. I never saw anyone drunk or even really tipsy. Daddy, who was very much the *Great Gatsby* type of man, would make mint juleps with fresh mint from the garden in his solid silver glasses rimmed with sugar frosting. If he had a beer, the golden liquid would be drunk from tulip-shaped, gold-rimmed pilsners.

That was one of my favorite things to see — how the beer looked in those glasses. I remember how pretty and sophisticated the mixed drinks looked. Later on, when I had my first mint julep, it tasted horrible, but it had certainly looked good from the outside.

My parents raised four children, and we looked like the picture-perfect family. I was the oldest.

I really idolized my father. He was so sophisticated. I remember very striking images of him. I can picture him working on his log cabin, which he later turned into a beautiful mansion. He wore khaki pants and a dungaree shirt, with a bandana ascot tucked into the shirt —a sharp-looking man. In another picture, I can see him as a man who was a fly fisherman because of the skill and sophistication that the sport required.

Father was supportive of me. I also felt he was honest with me. When he told me I was attractive or had good bone structure, I believed him. But if Mother told me those same things, I didn't believe her. I just thought she wanted something from me.

My mother wanted me to be what *she* wanted me to be. Since I was her oldest, she had plans for me right from the start. These plans were not in my scheme of things and therefore created tension between us and pressure on me.

I was a shy child. In fact, I was acutely shy — terrified of people. Mother wanted me to be a ballerina or a model, the most popular girl, or the winner of beauty contests. She pushed me very hard to achieve those things.

I was panic-striken at the thought of being on stage or dancing in front of people. I recall attending dancing school, but I either wouldn't dance or barely would. One of my worst memories was when she made me appear in a modeling show that she conducted. It was held at a movie theater. I walked downstage, did my turn, and was just dying inside. Then it was time to turn around and walk out. I had forgotten I couldn't really turn around and exit behind the curtain because there was a wall hidden behind the curtain. I panicked. I started frantically moving the curtain, searching for the break. Then Mother whispered a reminder to me to walk down the steps. I was absolutely mortified and humiliated. I never wanted to do anything like that again, and I didn't.

Mother tried to control me, but I fought her all the way. She told me when to shave my legs, when to start wearing makeup, when to get my first bra. I would follow along with her pushing part of the way, but then I would do as much as I could to screw things up.

I rebelled against her rule. I refused to be popular. I would run into the girl's room in school and rub off all the makeup she wanted me to wear. She'd invite people over expecting me to be outgoing and friendly, and I wouldn't say a word to them. Instead, I spent a great deal of time by myself listening to records or writing in the woods.

When I came home from college, things looked quite different at the house. Mother seemed a little more frantic and out of control. However, I didn't attribute her behavior to any cause. By that point I had started drinking, along with my artist husband-to-be. Alcohol and pot were a large part of his circle, so Mother's strange behavior was not regarded as being drug-related.

It wasn't until I was 21 or 22, married, and came home to escape my husband for a while that I saw Mother actually drunk. It was then that I realized how heavily she was drinking. She was acting absolutely off-the-wall. Drinking was taking over her life. She drank heavily every night.

She left Father to return to her childhood home. There she took up with a former beau who had remained single to take care of his mother. During that time, he had compiled a scrapbook on my mother. Mother yanked him up and ran off with him to New York City. It was a miserable marriage.

I was horrified at Mother's behavior. I don't think I've ever recovered from her drastic change. I felt my life up until that point had been a lie. I had had a fairly ideal childhood, aside from my shyness and battles with Mother. I had the parents everyone wanted. My parents had adored each other and our house had been filled with people. But Mother's late-blooming alcoholism blew everything apart.

I hated to see her drinking and drunk. Throughout my life Mother had always been supportive of me and had focused on me. But when I ran home to her with my own marriage faltering, she wasn't there anymore. She had left her marriage and was running around somewhere. When I finally caught up with her, she wasn't very pleased to see me. It was as if she were saying to me, "I don't want to hear about your problems. I want you to listen to mine."

Mother's drinking was a total betrayal of everything I had thought and believed. It devastated me.

What is now . . .

Five years ago I joined A.A. Prior to that time, I was definitely reaching my bottom. I had two beautiful children, a professor husband, and an ideal job — yet I couldn't get up off my sofa. I was drinking every day. I felt like everything was wrong, but I didn't know why.

One day, however, I figured out that my problems were related to my daily drinking. I went to a psychiatrist, but we were sidetracked on so many other issues that we never really confronted the drinking problem.

But I finally knew what I had to do. I visited an alcohol information center and listened when they told me about a hospital that treated problem drinkers on an outpatient basis. By next morning, I had made up my mind to go to the hospital. I drank five beers before I left, and was promptly admitted into a ten-day, inpatient program.

I learned about A.A. there, then attended some meetings when I got out. Although I did drink again, I finally went back to the program and stayed.

I didn't find out about Adult Children of Alcoholics meetings until I moved up north. My lover was an adult child, so I attended the meetings as a support person. As I listened at the meetings, I wondered why I was identifying with so many of the feelings. I related to the discussions about relationships with a manipulative parent. I identified with the controlling power Mother had had over me. I knew the feeling — firsthand — of trying to please someone who never seemed to be pleased.

I wondered if I qualified to be an adult child because there hadn't been any alcoholism in my formative years. After a few meetings, however, that question didn't seem to matter. By then, I was no longer attending meetings as a support to my lover, but as a support to myself.

What can be . . .

I still struggle with the program, with completely turning things over in my life to a Higher Power, and in doing the Steps. I still haven't done a Fourth Step in the program even though I've been in it for years. Yet I seem to be getting healthier, even if I'm going along at my slow pace.

I think I may have an easier job of recovery than most adult children because I didn't grow up with active drunks. For that, I am truly grateful, because I can't imagine how horrible life would've been knowing Mother's personality.

It's been interesting how my storybook family has turned out. Mother is a widow who is not drinking as heavily as she used to, but who is still an untreated alcoholic. My All-American brother, one who had everything from brains to brawn, is an alcoholic. My sister, who was the real Southern belle — homecoming queen and famous ballet dancer — has gone through five husbands. My other brother, a typical Mr. Chips, was voted the most-liked teacher in his school but is under the control of a domineering wife.

I'm the only one in the program. I realize now part of my downfall all the years prior to the program was in believing in the storybook appearances — the outside appearances — of my family. I know now just because my family looked like they should be in a television series didn't mean everything was okay. ACOA has helped me see beyond the surface to what's really underneath the exterior of the once-beautiful, idyllic life my parents had.

ACOA has also helped me see what's really underneath my own outside surface. To cover my shyness, I created an air of mystery around myself rather than an air of unsureness. Today I have, little by little, dropped some of that facade and let others see me for who I really am.

Being in the program and watching other people let themselves go have been helpful for me. Even though I still haven't completely let go, that can be a goal for me. Today, there's no turning back. I'm starting to face myself. I know now the belief that "She looks all right on the outside, so she must be all right" isn't true.

Now I'm ready to completely face myself. The program has unlocked me and helped me get out of myself. The program has set me free.

I AM A ROCK

Vinny's Story — Age: 40

Pain nourishes courage. You can't be brave if you've only had wonderful things happen to you.

— *Mary Tyler Moore*

I was labeled "The Rock" in the family because I was the one who assumed responsibilities when my father was drunk. I was the one who had to locate him on his drinking binges; I was the one who left football practice to assume his job; I was the one who had to manage his employees and handle finances when he shirked his role of business owner.

I grew up to be hard and controlled as a result. I brought those qualities into my marriage, where I continued to believe I should be the one in charge, the strong one, the one who provided. When my father died under tragic circumstances, I was the one who protected the family.

Yet I was helpless when it came to communicating with another human being. I didn't know what feelings were. I was so out of touch with the state of my marriage and couldn't understand what my wife meant when she said that things weren't right between us. The marriage ended. A short time later, I noticed a heavy drinking pattern in my daughter. I got scared.

When I started dating a woman who had an alcoholic parent and was attending ACOA meetings, my life changed for the better. She was becoming healthy, and I wanted some of that. I began going to the meetings and have seen my life improve ever since.

Today I'm still a rock in many ways, but now I have soft spots called feelings.

What once was . . .

From day one, my older brother was favored by my mother and I was favored by my father. My brother was reared to be the academic achiever; I was reared to become involved in my father's gas station business or in a similar trade.

As a result, I became very close to my father. In fact, I can honestly say he was my best friend and I was his. He included me in the fun things he did, like bowling and fishing. We built a boat together. I worked with him at his gas station for long hours. I listened to him when he confided in me, although sometimes this made me uncomfortable because he'd talk about his relationship with my mother. He didn't like her controlling behavior, the way she took charge of things in our lives, or how she'd put him down a lot.

But she had reasons for putting him down. My father was an alcoholic whose problem was evident to me by the time I was five or six years old. His drinking affected the entire family, from my brother and me to his brothers and sisters and close friends. Everyone saw what he was doing to his life and wanted to help him get off the booze. They would gather at our house to plead with my father to stop drinking and get his life together.

My aunt told me once that she used to discover empty liquor bottles under my father's pillow when he was in his early teens. That drinking pattern continued in his adult life. He would drink in social situations or would buy liquor and drink alone in a rented motel room. Other times he'd lock himself in the back room at his gas station and drink himself into a stupor. He'd growl, "Leave me alone!" to anyone who knocked on the door to see how he was. Even though he drank in private a good deal and never got himself into strange or uncontrollable situations, his alcoholism was taking its toll indirectly upon his business — and directly upon me.

Although I have a lot of good memories about our relationship, there are many bad ones too. I could see how his drinking affected his business because his condition determined whether or not he would be open or closed. He had to borrow money to make payroll and gasoline deliveries, and he got into many financial difficulties.

Aside from these problems in his business, his drinking had a direct effect on my life. I saw my best friend unable to take care of himself and his family. I felt responsible to him as a result, and over the years I developed an inner strength to protect him and rescue him.

When I was very young, I can remember trying to prevent him from killing himself. I was lying in bed one night, listening to my parents argue. I really wasn't paying attention to what they were saying until my father screamed out, "I'm going to jump out that window right now!" With that I bolted out of bed into their bedroom, grabbed my father, and hugged him. I cried out, "Don't, Dad, don't!" as I desperately hung onto him. My parents started crying, seeing me so upset. Then my father pulled me to him and said, "Vinny, I'm really not going to do that, but sometimes I get so angry and upset. " My father threatened suicide a number of times, and each time was very upsetting. I never really knew whether to believe him or not.

As I grew older, I literally had to put my father to bed when he came home from work because he couldn't make it up the stairs. In my early teenage years, I knew he had a severe problem. I began to fear liquor and made it my business to try to protect him as best I could.

My mother must have noticed the close relationship I had with him, because she put me in charge of handling my father when he was drunk. When he was off at some unknown location drinking, my mother would tell me I had to go find him and check on things at the gas station. That became the pattern for me over the years. I learned that the things I wanted to do had to be interrupted or put aside because of what my father was doing.

The interruptions could come at any time or when I was anywhere. My mother would track me down. I would feel such embarrassment during football practices when I'd be called off the field by my coach. My mother would be standing there, distraught and pleading, "Vinny, you have to come home. You have to go down to the gas station. Dad has gone someplace and you have to run the business. "

That's when I started putting my own needs and wishes aside to take care of everything and everyone else. I became a rescuer. I became hard and controlled. I was labeled "The Rock. "

I never knew, when I'd be called down to the station, whether I'd be working there a few hours, a day, a few days, a week, or a month. All I knew was I was in charge and if I didn't do the work my father was supposed to be doing, the business would fail. So there I was, at fourteen or fifteen years old, having total control over deliveries and employees. Utility companies would come to me and threaten to shut off the electricity because my father hadn't paid his bills. I had to wheel and deal with them while, at the same time, I had employees asking, "Vinny, what's going on?" The pressures were incredible, but I handled them. I'd bark at the workers, "Just shut up and do your work. Tune up that car!"

At night, I'd act out a lot. I'd put myself in physically dangerous situations. I got involved in a number of gang fights. I drove fast cars and motorcycles and carried a gun. I walked around with a rage inside of me but didn't know why. All I knew was I was very, very angry.

The relationship between my mother and father frustrated me a great deal. I was the go-between who was given the responsibility to help them patch things up. But that always had a way of working against me because I would usually end up being the focus of their anger. For example, on the night when my father threatened suicide and I ran into their bedroom so upset, I later heard them arguing over what had happened. My mother screamed accusingly at him, "Look what you've done to him! Look what you've done!" I then heard my father storm out of the house, and I felt very guilty about even trying to show him how much his threat affected me.

There were times when my father would be very belligerent and try to bait an argument with my mother. He'd pick and pick at her mercilessly. One night I couldn't stand it anymore, and I felt I had to protect her. I screamed, "Dad, will you shut up! Just shut up!" But instead of my mother being grateful for my intervention, she turned on me for telling my father to shut up. My father then grabbed me and yelled, "Don't talk to me like that or I'll break your back." At that point I was big enough to fight him, so I said, "Go ahead, make your move!" I was so confused. I couldn't understand why things got so crazy when I only wanted them to turn out good.

My life as a child wasn't always bad. When my father wasn't drinking, I would say I was very happy. I felt needed by my parents because of how I helped out. I enjoyed a popularity because of my father's owning a business in an inner city. There were many friends in my life.

But when my father drank, life was hell. I hated taking over his business. I hated being shouldered with the responsibility of trying to find him when he was off on a solitary drinking spree. I had to report to my mother every few hours in my search for him, and she would usually be very upset. She had visions of my finding him dead in an alley somewhere. Sometimes I also worried that I'd find him dead and have to report that to my mother. Little did I know that shortly after I left the house, that fear was to come true.

When I was 21 years old, I left the house to marry a woman I had been going with since I was sixteen. My father sold his gas station business because of physical and emotional pressures and started working as a facilities manager for one of his customers. He liked his job. He was even beginning to deal with his drinking problem. I had brought him up to a detox place for two weeks where he had dried out.

He had been living at home — sober — when I got a call from my mother one evening to say she was worried about my father. He had left home earlier to check on a new boiler at work and hadn't returned yet.

My first thought was maybe he had gone off drinking. I told my mother to wait for a while longer. She did, then called me back even more frantic. By that time he was overdue by several hours. I told her to call the police. I raced to the facility, feeling something was very wrong.

It was a cold night in January. When I arrived, the police hadn't yet gone into the building. As we got in, we all fanned out in different directions. I went with a police officer who was a friend of the family. I was with him when he found my father's body.

It looked like he had been shot in the head at close range. His head was a mess, all in pieces, and there was blood everywhere.

My first priority was to protect my father, just as I had done my whole life. In fact, I wouldn't let the officer I was with even come near his body. The minute we found him, I stood with my back to his body, facing anyone who tried to come near him. If necessary, I felt I would kill to protect him from any further injury.

The officer said gently, "Vinny, control yourself." I had to let the medical examiner and others through to view his body and the scene of the crime. I had a tough time letting them touch my father's body, but I drew the line at photographers. I didn't want newspapers to come into this because of my mother and the rest of the family. It was my responsibility to protect them.

The medical examiner told me my father hadn't been shot. He had been beaten to death, his head bludgeoned repeatedly.

I had to go home that night to tell my mother the news. I then called the rest of the family. Not once did I shed a tear. I was the rock for my father until the very end.

What is now . . .

I felt so many emotions other than rage at my father's murder. I felt responsible for his death. All I could think was if I had only been there, keeping him company as I sometimes did, he would still be alive.

When the police found the three kids who had beaten him to death, all I could feel was rage. I went to the courtroom with a loaded gun concealed under my jacket. I sat directly behind the three of them, and I could imagine myself popping them right off — one, two, three. The only thing that prevented me from doing that was the love I had for my daughter and wife. I didn't want any more problems than those we already had.

Our marriage was far from perfect. Much of the tension in the relationship came from me and the issues I had brought into it from my childhood. I felt I had to be the rock, always in control of the situation. I had to be the responsible one, providing well for my family. I gave them material things they didn't even want, but I felt we must have in order to look like we had a good marriage.

I worked two jobs and went to night school, not for myself, but for our appearance as a family. I took charge and struggled to always go one more step to acquire all the "nice things" I felt were important.

But I wasn't in touch with any inner feelings or communication. I didn't really have any sensitivity toward another human being's feelings and needs. Hurt, pain, and the need to be the strong one had stripped me of that awareness. At all costs, I wanted to avoid any behaviors that were at all like my alcoholic father's.

One day, my wife told me our marriage wasn't right, and it wasn't working. I didn't know what she was talking about because I felt I was doing everything I was supposed to and we had all the things I thought we should have.

We divorced and shared custody of our daughter, who was twelve, and our son, who was eight. I loved them both, and that's why I was so shaken when my daughter came home drunk. I immediately felt fear and called my ex-wife. "Do you know that she's drinking?" I asked. My wife then confirmed to me that my daughter had been drinking before.

That night, my daughter threw up and passed out in bed. I sat next to her through most of the night, stroking her hair, watching her sleep, and praying that her drinking wouldn't develop into a problem like it had for my father.

But her drinking continued. There was a great deal of commotion around the house whenever she was drunk, and it reminded me of how things had been in my childhood home. I didn't know what to do. I dealt with a lot of those feelings in therapy, but rarely confronted my issues as an adult child.

I started dating a woman who also had an alcoholic parent. In the beginning of our relationship, if she saw me with a beer in hand, she'd start to get very uptight and ask me whether or not I was an alcoholic. We talked a little bit about our feelings growing up in an alcoholic home, but not really in too much detail.

Then she started to attend an Adult Children of Alcoholics group. At first all I could think of was that the group was a bunch of goody-goodies. I believed I was handling my issues just fine in therapy and didn't need a group of strangers to help me out. I had visions of Adult Children of Alcoholics being a bunch of people hugging and kissing and "getting in touch" like a 1960s hippie movement.

But over time I changed my opinion because she began to change. She started getting healthy. She was starting to smile and talk about her feelings and seemed more confident than she had ever been. As a result, our relationship seemed to be improving.

Finally, I went with her one time to a meeting, just out of curiosity, to see how those meetings were helping her be more open and honest. What I saw and heard there was part of a very good experience for me. I discovered that the group was nothing like therapy. It was just a group of people with common issues who were helping each other in a communal way.

For my first six meetings, all I did was sit and listen. Finally, I had enough courage to speak. Over time, through listening and sharing, I started to feel really good after the meetings. I started to feel like I had been to confession and all my sins had been forgiven. I felt lighter.

I heard many things coming out of people's mouths at the meetings that I too could have been saying. I gained a great deal of courage from the meetings. I started to show and express my feelings.

What can be . . .

The more I attend ACOA meetings, the more I realize there's not a hell of a lot of difference between members of Adult Children of Alcoholics. The names may be different, the number of people in the family may vary, but we are all struggling with the same issues.

The fact that my father was murdered made me no different from any other adult child in the meetings I attended. I learned the circumstances of my childhood aren't as important as the feelings I have. Those are what can be identified, shared, and rectified.

I've made many changes since I've been in the program. In my relationship with my daughter, I've learned to let go and let her work through her own disease. I can't stop her drinking by chaining her to her room when she stays with me. Only she can deal with her disease. All I can do is pray for her and support her as best as I can, but detach from her when her behavior is unacceptable.

In my relationship with my girlfriend, I'm more honest now with my feelings. Instead of covering things up as I've done in the past, I've confronted things more openly and honestly.

Today I'm more aware of my feelings and the feelings of those around me. I cry in theaters now when I feel sadness. I even cry in front of my kids. I'm still a rock because it feels comfortable for me to be that way. But I'm more willing to share my emotions with other people now and to admit I'm human.

I think one of the areas that's been most difficult for me to deal with has been my father's death. But the program is helping me with that. I've learned there are certain things in my life I cannot change. I cannot change a person who is an alcoholic, nor can I bring my father back.

I accept the loss of him. Today, if I could talk to him, I would want to tell him how much I appreciate and understand what alcohol can do to a person — as beautiful a person as he was. I've seen how alcohol can just take hold of a person and rule him.

The program has helped me cope with the loss of my father through acceptance. The next step for me now is forgiveness. That will be more difficult for me to learn, for I still fantasize from time to time about "an eye for an eye and a tooth for a tooth."

But I've learned, through others in the program, that hanging onto anger is so much harder. It's easier to smile than to walk around wearing a frown. The rock in me wants the frown to remain, hard and cold. But there is a soft spot in that rock that recognizes the truth of the program: It is easier to forgive and get on with my life in the present, rather than to look backward. I know that soon I'll meet forgiveness on the path I'm walking today.

THE INVISIBLE "ISM"

Katie's Story — Age: 36

There are three things that only God knows: the beginning of things, the cause of things, and the end of things.

— Welsh Proverb

Looking back, I often wonder when and where everything began. When did I start having overpowering feelings of anxiety and fear? Where did I acquire such low self-esteem? When did I learn that nothing I ever did would be good enough? Where did I learn how to people-please for love and approval?

When I first began to attend Adult Children of Alcoholics meetings, I heard people talk of the disease of alcoholism and the parent or parents who drank. But I never had any visible, active alcoholism. So why, I began to wonder, could I relate to all fourteen qualifying questions of an adult child of an alcoholic?

Today I feel I belong to Adult Children of Alcoholics, even though neither my mother nor my father was an alcoholic. I have learned that the disease of alcoholism isn't always visible. Just because someone doesn't drink doesn't mean the person is free of the disease of alcoholism. Through attending both Al-Anon and ACOA meetings, I was made aware of alcoholism as a threefold disease: physical, mental, and spiritual. Just because *alcohol* isn't visible doesn't mean that the *ism* isn't there. It's just invisible.

Sometimes I wish I had concrete reasons for the issues I'm working on right now. Oftentimes I sit at an ACOA meeting and can't relate to descriptions of drunken, alcoholic parents and their behaviors.

But what I can relate to are the feelings, no matter whose story I'm listening to. I know now that's what it's all about — the feelings. What I lack in a visible alcoholic background I certainly make up in the intensity of feeling I carry around today.

What once was . . .

I was the oldest of three children. My brother and sister fought constantly, but I rarely did. I don't think I ever wanted to fight or disagree with anyone, for I was afraid I wouldn't be liked. Since that meant so much to me, I was very easy to get along with. I rarely made a fuss or tried to call attention to myself or my needs. I was a timid child, compliant, and ready to please. I was also a very frightened, anxious, fear-filled little girl.

My mother did very little to calm these feelings. My relationship with her was always difficult. I struggled desperately to please her, to try to win her approval of me and to get her to love me. Yet no matter what I did or how well I did, nothing ever seemed right.

One of those areas of right and wrong was my feelings. My mother taught me that my feelings were not normal. I learned not to show them, feel them, talk about them, or deal with them.

I recall intense anxiety prior to my First Communion. I was nervous and shaking as I put on my new outfit. As time got closer to our departure for the church, my fears built into an anxiety attack. I felt faint and thought I was going to be sick. I told my mother. She replied that I'd be fine, then shoved me out on the back porch to "get some air."

There I stood, alone and frightened, gulping in air at the back door. My feelings didn't seem to go away at all by getting the air; in fact, I felt even worse than when I was in the house. Somehow I remember leaving for the church and getting through the ceremony. But at no time did my mother ever tell me that nervous, anxious feelings are okay to have before a formal event.

As a result, my fears always escalated whenever unusual or unexpected events occurred. One time my mother enrolled me in the school lunch program, even though I normally came home for lunch. When I came downstairs that morning, she announced, "Katie, you're not coming home today for lunch." My heart started beating faster, and I felt very scared. I think I worked myself up so badly that I was too nervous to even eat my lunch at school.

Over time, I gradually learned not to share my feelings with my mother. She and I were very much alike in that respect. I learned how to suppress my feelings just as she did. Rarely would she show any feelings, particularly anger. We kids learned after a while that when our mother was angry, she would start to frantically clean the house. We would watch her tearing through the house, look at each other and think, "Oh, Mom's mad at something."

There were some happy times in my childhood. Those times involved the family as a whole unit, not just my mother and me. When she and my father were together, I remember I used to get a warm feeling inside just looking at them. All of us would have wonderful times together when we'd vacation. For many years we rented the same lakeside place.

I also had a great time whenever I was with my dad. He and I had a close relationship that I think was quite special. He wasn't like my mother at all. He cared about my feelings and listened to me when I talked to him. He was very supportive of me and didn't criticize the way I did things. His acceptance was a refreshing change from my mother's criticism.

There were many things missing in my childhood. One of them was an acceptance of my abilities and limitations. I felt a great deal of disappointment at the fact that nothing I did was ever good enough for my mother. I remember I would complete a project and run in to show her. Instead of seeing the work I had done on it, she was ready to criticize. "Why did you do that in blue, Katie?" she'd question, or "It would've been so much nicer if you'd done it this way." The times when I was really proud or excited about something I had done, I never seemed to get the response from her that I needed. After a while, I gave up. I believed anything I did would never be good enough.

My feelings of low self-esteem strongly affected my high school years. I wanted very much to take business courses in high school and planned for a career in the business world. However, the principal told me I couldn't take business classes because my IQ was too high. Rather than disagree with her or push for what I wanted, I complied with her wishes and took four years of college courses. I never once realized I had any choice in the matter. I believed, as at home, I shouldn't rock the boat or else I wouldn't be liked. I also believed the principal knew my capabilities more than I did. If she said I wasn't right for business, I must not be.

Those four years were a waste for me. I stayed at the bottom track of the smart kids. I never excelled in any subject because I really wasn't interested. But as it later turned out, I graduated from high school and attended a secretarial college. There, I was an A student and won a scholarship. But not once during high school did I ever tell anyone, "This isn't what I want to do for me!"

I brought a background filled with compliance and low self-esteem into my marriage. I thought everything was going to be a fairy tale come true and everyone would live happily ever after. Even though my husband had lost his first wife and was raising a young son, I knew I made him happy. I felt I could continue to make him happy in our marriage.

But I was unprepared for the events that were to occur in the first years of my marriage. Although my childhood hadn't been idyllic, it had been crisis-free. There had been no deaths or accidents or major illnesses. Despite the stress and suppressed feelings, my childhood home had run smoothly. I believed the rest of the world ran that way too.

But the marriage taught me something different. First, my husband was an alcoholic. Even though his drinking was very bad at one point, I denied any hurt or pain I felt as a result of his drinking and his behaviors. In fact, the minute he walked through the door I was ready to forgive and forget. I would think, "There. He's here. That's all that matters." I wouldn't get angry at him or acknowledge that his behaviors had affected me at all.

Added to my husband's drinking was our decision to start our family right away. Within three months of our marriage, I got pregnant. Our four children were born in a five-year span. My husband's drinking, combined with the pressures of taking care of four children, brought about behaviors in me that were reminiscent of my mother's coping mechanisms.

I began to clean house like I was doing battle against a foe. I believed we needed to look great to the outside world. I was a wreck because I neglected taking care of me, but couldn't imagine ignoring the house. Cleaning became an obsession for me. I set incredibly strict rules that governed when beds were to be made, when laundry had to be done, rugs vacuumed, sheets changed, lawn mowed, and dishes cleaned. At the time, these rules didn't seem extreme.

Things could have gone along that way for quite a while if a major tragedy hadn't brought me up short. One of our sons died at six weeks of Sudden Infant Death Syndrome (SIDS). His death started my decline into a bottom that would go on for a couple of years.

I remember how I handled his death. He died on a Thursday. We buried him on a Friday. It was Memorial Day weekend. By Monday, everything was over as if it had never happened. It was as if he had never existed.

That feeling drove me crazy. Close friends didn't acknowledge his life or his death to me. I carried incredible pain around for a while.

Then, a year and a half later, I got pregnant again. I was absolutely terrified. When our youngest son was born, I was in sheer panic for the first few days. I didn't want to feel any love for this child because I didn't want to get hurt. But, as his mother, that was difficult to do.

When he came home from the hospital, I was a nervous wreck. He was sleeping peacefully through the night, but I wasn't. I would get up almost every hour or so and go into his room to make sure he was breathing. Soon, I became physically and emotionally worn out. I experienced illnesses and pains. Sometimes I would even be doubled over from the pain in my stomach. Other times I would be suffering with migraines.

I saw doctors about my pains. A gynecologist recommended a hysterectomy for my abdominal pains, and I consented to surgery. Then I made an appointment with a neurologist to find a cure for my migraines. After he examined me he suggested I go to a psychotherapist, which I did.

I remember telling my family at the time that the insurance we had would cover eleven weeks with a psychotherapist. I told them I was certain I'd be fine in eleven weeks.

What is now . . .

After about ten months of talking about my fears and worries with the psychotherapist, she suggested I try Al-Anon. That was six years ago, and I've been going regularly since that time.

The first meeting gave me a connectedness that therapy hadn't given me. I felt nine feet tall when I left that meeting. All I could think was, "I am not crazy after all. I am not crazy." I knew I belonged, right from the beginning.

After I had been in Al-Anon for a while, my father became terminally ill. I think that if I didn't have the Al-Anon program at the time, I never could've gotten through his final time with me. Everyone else in my family was into their usual suppression and denial of the reality of what was going on, believing my father would recover. But I knew I had to deal with the reality of his eventual death, which I did.

I spent a good deal of time with him, even though I had my children and husband to care for. But the program taught me that I needed to recognize my needs. Even though I felt, from time to time, the tugs of "What I should be doing," I ended up doing what I felt I needed to do.

In time, as my father's illness grew worse, I took on the role of parent, and he of child. I took him shopping. I helped him into bed. I tried to be there for him emotionally the way he had been there for me when I was a child.

His death was a turning point for me. For one thing, I felt better about myself as a person because I had dealt with the reality of his death. I never once denied what would inevitably happen to him. I learned from his death that I could trust my own judgment to believe what I needed to believe.

After my father's death, I became involved in a bereavement workshop. There, I discovered I had already done much of the grief work for my father before he died. Surprisingly, I realized I was dealing with my mother in the workshop. I was grieving the emotional support she had never been able to give me.

When I finished the workshop, my Al-Anon sponsor told me about an Adult Children of Alcoholics meeting she was attending. She said to me, "Katie, it seems a good deal of your issues are really adult children issues. I think you need to try some ACOA meetings."

When I first went to ACOA meetings, I really didn't think I belonged there. The only alcoholic in my life I could identify was my husband, and I already had Al-Anon to deal with him.

But I could answer yes to all fourteen qualifying questions for an adult child. I could certainly relate to how it felt to grow up in an alcoholic home. The only way my life was different was in the invisibility of the alcohol.

What can be . . .

ACOA meetings helped me in many ways. First, they gave me the ability to parent myself — to learn how to reach out to get the emotional support I need. Through ACOA, I've met some wonderful people who are caring and supportive of the things I do in my life.

The program is also helping me learn how to be a better mother. Before, I had behaved the same way with my children that my mother had with me. I criticized their little projects, found fault, and gave little praise. I could never show my feelings as a role model for them or validate the ones they had because I didn't know how. But ACOA is helping me change all that. I'm acquiring some valuable mothering skills just by talking and listening to others.

I'm also grateful to the program for helping me learn how to mother my stepson. Our relationship has always been difficult because the loss of his mother has made him afraid of getting close to me. The tools in the program have been useful for me in detaching from him. Now I am not so caught up in the fact that I believe I could be a good mother to him if only he'd let me. I know now how to let go of him and let my Higher Power help me with our relationship.

The program has also given me the courage to pursue a career. When I started in ACOA, I was a clerk. But I wanted to better myself. After I had been in the program a while, my sponsor told me about a school that gave credit for students' life experiences. To qualify, I had to document my life experience in a formal portfolio.

Putting that portfolio together was unbelievably difficult for me because I had to reflect on my life and recollect where I had come from. But I realized when it was completed just how much work I had done through therapy and the program. I learned I had come a long, long way from the person who attended her first meeting years before.

Now I have only a month of school left. Even though I'm scared and don't really know where I'm going, I realize one very special thing. No one can take this away from me. It's all mine. And I did it all not because I'm somebody's mother or somebody's wife — I did it because I'm me.

I think the greatest gift of the program is that it can make life very manageable. Through ACOA, I have been able to look at priorities. One of them is taking care of myself. It used to be that I would be the last person I would think of because everyone else would come first.

Now I can put myself in line, along with everyone else. Sometimes I'm first, sometimes I'm second, and sometimes I'm even at the end of the line. But, because I care about myself and my needs, I know now when to call my needs a priority and deal with them in a unselfish way.

Through this self-care, I am no longer invisible.

NEVER NURTURED

Rene's Story — Age: 34

The hardest thing you will ever have to do is trust your own gut and find what seems to work for you.

— Barbara Walters

I wish I could point to alcoholism today and say, "There! That was the cause of all of my childhood problems." But I can't. Alcoholism existed in the family, but I was not brought up in a home that was ruled by it.

My childhood was filled with two dysfunctional parents. My father had a criminal record; my mother suffered from severe depression. When I was very young, my mother went to the state hospital for treatment. My father gave my siblings and me to an aunt and uncle.

My uncle was a recovering alcoholic. My aunt made it perfectly clear from the start she didn't want us. Her overt rejection, combined with my father's abandonment and my mother's illness, made me feel very insecure. I felt unloved and unnurtured.

When I was much older, I started to be affected by my father's drinking. I began attending Al-Anon meetings, but felt something was missing from my life. I had difficulty maintaining relationships. I carried around parcels of anger and rage that overburdened me.

When I first discovered Adult Children of Alcoholics, I was very frightened. I identified too much with others. But, as I began to attend meetings regularly and communicate my feelings, I began to discover what I had missed all my life — caring and support in a safe atmosphere. For the first time in my life, I discovered through ACOA what it felt like to be nurtured.

What once was . . .

What I remember most about my childhood is the silence. Almost from the time I was in the crib, nothing was ever talked about, shared, discussed, aired, or brought up between any family members.

On the night my mother was taken away, my younger brother and I were together in a crib in a corner of a room in my aunt's house. My mother had been out of control that night, acting hysterically. I was very scared because I didn't understand what was happening. All I knew was my mother was being taken away. No one said anything to me.

My father left my older brother and sister and my younger brother and me at my aunt and uncle's. They were our appointed guardians. I remember being told we were lucky to be kept together as a family while my parents were away, but I didn't feel lucky at all.

I could see no reason why we couldn't stay with my father until my mother got better and came home. I interpreted his leaving us to mean he didn't want us anymore. First my mother, then my father seemed to walk away from us with no real explanation given. I always seemed to be asking the questions, "Where is my mother? Where is my father?"

Until I was nine, my aunt and uncle served as my parents. They had raised seven children of their own, but only two were in the house while I was there. One child was filled with anger all the time. The other was twenty years old, overly sensitive, and highly emotional. I thought the kids were normal.

My uncle was a recovering alcoholic who was pretty nice to my younger brother and me because we were cute little boys, but my aunt didn't really like us or want us there. In fact, I once overheard her say to my uncle that she didn't want us there. I didn't like living with them. I felt very underloved and undernurtured.

I did feel grateful at the time for my aunt and uncle's generosity. But I later found out my father had paid them to take care of us. That made me feel even worse about living with them. It felt like nobody really wanted me or my siblings.

My mother came home after seven years of treatment. We were reunited as a family once again — Mother, Father, and children. For a brief period of time the home felt very settled. I remember thinking, "Oh, great! Now everything's going to be all right. Everything's going to be perfect." My mother was a perfectionist, and that control felt very comfortable to me at first.

Her perfectionism, however, got to a point that bordered on fanaticism. If things weren't done just right, she would erupt into a big explosion and rage. This usually was followed by tears. Both of my parents shared in that rage. They shared equally in violent bouts of screaming and uncontrolled tempers. I never knew when these scenes would happen or why.

My father took a great deal of his anger out on my younger brother. He blamed him for a lot of things — one of them, my mother's breakdown. Since she had to be hospitalized after his birth, my father believed my brother to be the reason for her breakdown. At one point, my dad wanted to give him up for adoption to a cousin in the family, but my mother found out about it and prevented it. But that didn't stop my dad from making him suffer. He mostly used steady verbal abuse, along with spankings that bordered on violent hitting.

Many times the angry outbursts would occur over the tension-filled dinner table. One night, during an argument, my father's criminal record was revealed. The silence about his past was broken. I was twelve years old. After that, whenever anything in the house would be missing, my mother would blame my father, but the guilty parties would be me or my younger brother.

I grew up feeling very depressed. I remember sitting outside on some steps when I was about six years old, crying my eyes out. Inside I was wishing really hard that someone would come along and hold me. Just hold me and tell me everything would be better. I wanted a fairy godmother to appear and take care of me and nurture me for ever and ever. Then I would live happily ever after.

Years of wishing and never having the wish come true started to harden me. I stopped wishing and started telling myself I didn't need anyone to care about me or nurture me. I knew no one really cared up until that point in time, so I couldn't imagine things changing. I felt more and more bitter inside. I began to see myself as a freak — a really unlovable, uncared for person. That image hurt, but I didn't know how else to see myself.

I coped by trying to be invisible. I had very few friends. The few friends I did have I chose because they came from similar backgrounds. They were children from split homes or alcoholic parents. They were more soulmates than they were friends. I felt comfortable around them because they were just as bad off as I was. I figured they wouldn't look down on me the way I believed everyone else did.

When I was in my sophomore year of high school, I found a different way to cope with my insecurities and pain. I started getting involved in drugs. I thought drugs were great. They seemed to parallel the way I felt about myself. I started with pot, then any pill someone would hand me. I even tried heroin.

Drugs took the edge off of everything. They made it easier for me to cope with the low self-image I had. I also started drinking, just like my older brother had done. When my younger brother was fifteen, he got even heavier into drugs than I had, with acid his drug of choice.

Each of us coped in his own way.

When I was sixteen years old, my mother was diagnosed as having cancer. She had a hysterectomy and a mastectomy, but the cancer spread to her chest, lungs, and throat. She was dying.

No one talked about her illness. She went into the hospital for regular radium treatments, but no one was really in touch with what was going on to be able to offer her support. I think there was a lot of denial going on about the cancer. No one talked about her illness. No one really knew how she was feeling. Life seemed to go on in its usual fashion. My father was away from the house more than he was there because of his workaholism. That left my siblings and myself on our own.

I, for one, wasn't aware of the extent of her illness. It wasn't until the night before she died that I finally understood her disease was going to win. I visited her in the hospital. Her sickness was graphically evident to me. She was bloated and being kept alive by machines and tubes. I couldn't believe what I was seeing.

I tried to tell her I loved her, but it wouldn't come out. Instead, I ran into the hospital corridor sobbing hysterically. Somehow I found a pay phone and some change. I dialed home and got my sister on the phone. At first she couldn't understand me because I was blubbering incoherently through my hysterical crying. When I was able to calm down a little I screamed at her, "Why didn't anyone tell me? Mom's really sick. I think she's going to die!" My sister replied very calmly, "Oh yeah. She's been dying, y'know."

The next morning, while I was lying in bed, my father told me my mother had died during the night. I pulled the covers over my head. I didn't want to hear it or believe it.

What is now . . .

Throughout my adult life, I held onto three predominant emotions: rage, depression, and hysteria. Those influenced me in all I did.

One of the areas in my adulthood that was the most difficult for me to deal with was a sexual relationship. I would cling to the other person like a drowning person to a life preserver. I felt I really *needed* the other person for my survival. My greatest fear was to be abandoned. I brought into each relationship I had a desperate, nervous tension that only served to contribute to the impermanence of the relationship. It became only a matter of time before the relationship ended.

When that happened, I took the ending as a statement that I was once again unworthy and unlovable. But instead of letting anyone see the pain I was in, I treated the termination with indifference. I withheld my emotions from other people, as well as from myself. I told myself that person didn't matter.

When I started a new relationship, my characteristics would be there once again. And, once again, the relationship would be doomed to fail.

When I was 33 years old, I started to identify the pattern I was bringing into my relationships. I wanted to do something to change, so I began to see a therapist. We started the sessions by discussing my relationships. As time went on, however, I began to open up about different subjects. One had to do with my father. I had been spending some time with him and had noticed he was drinking a great deal. Once I started talking about his use of alcohol, that opened many doors for me to talk about my childhood.

I started to attend Al-Anon meetings because I blamed myself for my father's drinking. I felt he needed me and I should be more supportive of him. He didn't have a wife or children in the house anymore. Why shouldn't I let him live with me? Why shouldn't I be taking care of him? I believed those were the reasons behind his drinking and it was up to me to do something about them.

Al-Anon helped me with the powerlessness I had over his drinking. But I didn't know what to do about the rage and anger I felt inside. I didn't know where to go to get help with that.

One night I got my answer. I mistakingly attended an Adult Children of Alcoholics meeting, thinking it was an Al-Anon meeting. What I heard that night I couldn't believe. I felt very paranoid in that meeting. I thought it was a setup for me. The things they were talking about were exactly what I had been feeling inside, but hadn't yet voiced. How did they know how I was feeling? How did all those people know I'd attend that meeting?

The whole room seemed to shrink in on me with each minute I sat there and listened. The fourteen questions read at the beginning of the meeting were a perfect profile of me. I was shocked. I was scared. I couldn't cope with the identification I felt that night.

I didn't go back to an Adult Children of Alcoholics meeting for a long time.

What can be . . .

When I ran from that first ACOA meeting, I was running away from all the fears I had about breaking silence, talking about feelings, and not denying anymore. I didn't know how to live without silence and denial, yet I knew I must if I was ever going to grow and get healthier. But it was only when I felt ready to challenge my fears that I attended ACOA meetings again on a regular basis.

Recovery began for me when I started opening my mouth in meetings. Instead of running from the list of fourteen questions, I accepted them by saying, "This is who you are, Rene." The next step was for me to learn what to do about who I was.

I knew I felt an overdeveloped sense of responsibility toward my father, which I had to deal with first before I could even begin to start working on myself.

I had to let go of my father. So I made him aware of the program without getting all wrapped up in trying to make his life better for him. I helped him by making program tools available to him, but it was up to him to pick them up and start to make his own repairs. I even told him I loved him. I had never told him that before, and I had a great deal of fear about admitting that emotion to him. Even though he didn't respond to me in kind when I told him, it still felt great. I realized I was doing my half in a relationship with him. That was all I could do. It was up to him to do his half in order to make the relationship work.

The important thing about telling him I loved him was I did it with no expectations, no hopes, and no wishful thinking that things would be all right after all. I didn't tell him to make up for all the nurturing I'd missed when I was growing up. I told him simply because I felt it.

Through the program, I've discovered I need to learn to do a lot of my own nurturing. I've started to work on my self-esteem. I take one of my fears, challenge it, and work through it as best I can until I gain a little more confidence and grow out of my fear. Then I take another fear and do the same thing.

The rewards are incredible. In the relationship I'm presently in, I now have some of my own personal power. I don't feel as desperate as I have been in the past. I'm putting trust and security into the relationship, and that's what I'm getting back.

Today I'm not afraid if the relationship ends. I'm a part of it — an equal part. Every day is different, and I now want to sit back and enjoy the relationship rather than possess it and clutch onto it as if I need it to save me.

The trust I now have in myself is there because of the new sense of spirituality I have. The program put me in touch with a Higher Power that's out there watching over me and taking care of me. I'm sure of this Power because twice, when I've knelt down to pray, I've had my prayers answered. That gives me a great deal of confidence knowing I'm believed in. It helps me to believe in me.

There are so many people who believe in me now. The ACOA group has been wonderful, nurturing me and helping me to understand who I am. I've discovered I'm a human being. I'm accepted and loved in the group. I'm never judged nor condemned for anything I think or feel.

I don't let those wonderful feelings of nurturing and caring stay inside of the group, only at meetings. I've been able to take those confident feelings into many parts of my life.

Today I've discovered that with just a little nurturing, I am growing by leaps and bounds. That's all I need to give me the confidence to conquer my fears and live my life to the fullest.

MISS GOODY TWO SHOES

Anne's Story — Age: 38

We are haunted by an ideal life, and it is because we have within us the beginning and the possibility of it.

— *Phillips Brooks*

My mother and father were children of alcoholics. While neither of them exhibited alcoholic drinking while I was growing up, they did exhibit all the symptoms of the disease of alcoholism.

There was considerable chaos in my home, an incredible amount of anger, and constant criticism. I was the fixer and the hero around the house. At school, I joined many extracurricular activities to gain my parents' approval. Yet nothing I did seemed to make a difference to my parents. I never really got their approval.

My sisters treated me as an outsider because they interpreted my approval seeking as being a Miss Goody Two Shoes. I felt isolated and alone. No one accepted me for who I was. No one wanted to give — or receive — love, affection, and nurturing.

Later I married an alcoholic and life continued to be chaotic. He went into treatment and I attended therapy groups for spouses of alcoholics. In those groups, counselor after counselor told me I was an adult child of an alcoholic. At first I couldn't understand why, but once I started going to ACOA meetings, I realized my parents didn't have to drink in order to qualify as alcoholics. What mattered was their behavior.

In my own recovery, I found out my behavior mattered. Through ACOA, I learned I didn't have to seek constant approval to feel good about myself as a person. I learned I didn't have to be Miss Goody Two Shoes anymore. All I had to be was me.

What once was . . .

Everything I did while I was growing up was designed to please my father. I adored him, but my fear of him seemed to overpower that. I felt he could kill me if he wanted to. He was intimidating by his physical size and by an incredibly fiery anger that could ignite at any moment, without prior warning. That meant he could turn on me at any time.

Sometimes my mother had prior knowledge of his temperament and could forewarn me. But many times I wouldn't have that warning, and I'd have to discover his mood on my own. I remember one time I saw him holding a pan over my mother's head — ready to hit her — because he was infuriated by something she had done. His size, as well as his out-of-control behavior, was frightening to see.

At other times, I might approach him to ask him for five dollars. For no visible reason, he'd start a tirade directed at my character. He'd scream I was no good, a lazy bum, and a rotten person. What had I possibly done to deserve five dollars? he'd demand. Yet at other times, using the same approach, he'd freely give me ten dollars without an unkind word.

On any given day, I never knew what his mood would be. Something he had seen on television might trigger an angry mood. A headache could set him off, or even some work pressures. I just had to take my chances whenever I approached him.

Despite his temper and constant criticism, I have some wonderful memories of growing up with him. He was really the only one who was there for my older sisters, my younger brother, and me. Intellectually and emotionally, he was the one I went to whenever I had a problem. He'd at least offer advice and seem to be interested in helping.

He was very focused on the family and the things we did together. He took us ice skating. He taught us about religion and how to swim. He gave us skiing lessons and arranged wonderful plane trips over lakes. We were a very musical family, and he took a major role in encouraging us to exhibit our musical talents. He bought a summer house that he dragged us to on summer vacations.

While he could be fun to be with, we still paid a price. We were constantly reminded about how he did everything for us.

I felt a lot of love for my mother, but mostly because I pitied her. She was a very depressed person who needed to be taken care of. She wasn't very proud of the way she looked, and that certainly showed. Her hair was a mess, and she rarely took care of personal hygiene like brushing her teeth regularly. Rarely would she buy any new clothes for herself. Around the house she wore horrible clothing. But on Saturday nights, she could make herself look gorgeous when she and my father were going out for dinner.

My mother spent a great deal of her life doing two things: believing she was able to control everyone's behavior and being depressed. My mother had a very low sense of self-esteem that she chose to share with me frequently. I always felt sorry for her.

At first I didn't like the role of being a listening ear to my mother. Over time, however, I grew to appreciate the attention she paid to me. When my sisters rejected me, my mother would always be there. I became her little pet and friend. She'd tell me, "I know. They're jealous of you because you do things well and they don't. But never you mind. You're a good little girl." I felt very comforted by my mother at those times. Yet I still didn't feel accepted.

I grew up feeling I had worked overtime to people-please. I couldn't just be a cheerleader, I had to be the best cheerleader on the squad. I couldn't just be a good student, but I had to make all the teachers like me better than anyone else in the class. Academically, I wasn't an outstanding student, so I tried to overachieve in other ways.

I joined Glee Club after Glee Club because I knew how important music was to my father. I eventually became president of one because I wanted to please him. I felt being bubbly and cute, a cheerleader, and Glee Club president would please Daddy.

I was starting to earn the reputation of being a Miss Goody Two Shoes at school. I was a good girl who tried to do everything right. Yet nobody really knew the inner struggles I was having. I was always trying to prove myself. I never felt comfortable with myself or good about myself. I never felt confident in my abilities or satisfied with my achievements. I felt I could always do more or that I could do it better.

At home I tried to fix the family and make everything better. During my father's angry tirade at my mother when he held a pan over her head to hit her, I jumped in between them. I started crying as I looked into my father's eyes. He didn't hit my mother that time; I sometimes felt very powerful that I could influence his angry behavior.

I felt if I was the nicest person I could possibly be, did all the "right" things, and pleased everyone, things would work out okay and everything would be better. I felt it was all up to me.

I remember how desperately I wanted our family to be together and share as a family. I wanted things to be fair and asked for family meetings, but we never had a discussion about it.

My sisters watched me get my parents' approval for my extracurricular activities and my Goody Two Shoes attitude. My middle sister used anger as her weapon, while my older sister became very depressed and slept a lot. Both of them started to resent me as I was growing up. If

I tried to be included with them while they were together, I'd get a door slammed in my face. I'd hear them laughing at me behind the door, and I'd feel miserable.

I carried some of that misery into my friendships. I seemed to unconsciously choose to be friends with two people who were already close to each other. I accepted the subservient, outsider role in those trios, just like I did with my sisters.

No matter how much of a "good girl" I was, things never seemed to get better at home. There was always constant criticism and almost daily arguments. The house was chaotic. My parents would start on projects and never finish them. Rules were made and then broken.

Dinnertime was probably the most chaotic time of all. There were two things I could always count on: the meal would be at precisely 5:30, and there would always be total chaos and tension. At those times, not only would there be personal criticisms of the children and my mother, but also angry tirades directed at politicians, communists, nuclear warfare, rapists, and kidnappers. I grew up hating mealtimes and fearing all the terrible things in the world I was told could happen to me.

I felt bad that I couldn't help things get better at home. I carried that guilt with me everywhere. If something good happened to me, I'd feel guilty. I might be asked out on a date with a boy I really liked. I'd feel good for a short time, then start to feel really badly about all the other people who weren't happy like I was. I then accepted responsibility for their happiness. I'd apologize to a friend and say, "Things will start to get better for you, too."

I never knew how to enjoy the good things that would happen to me. I even felt guilty for things I didn't do. If someone in a classroom was charged with stealing an item, I'd start to blush. I automatically felt guilty and sometimes wondered if I really had stolen the item. But I was Miss Goody Two Shoes, so I never would have stolen anything.

What is now . . .

When I was growing up, my father would express open affection only after he had had something to drink. I didn't like those times, even though he'd be really easy to get along with, because I didn't trust him then. I knew when he didn't have a drink he'd be his same, unpredictable self.

Even though my parents had had alcoholism in their families of origin, there was practically no discussion of their childhoods. Their mothers were usually sweet or wonderful, while the fathers were rarely mentioned.

Yet my parents clearly had no sense of themselves as individuals and no self-esteem. As a result, I grew up with no adult role model. When I married an alcoholic and spent several years trying to make consistency out of chaos, adult life seemed normal. I began to exhibit the same out-of-control behaviors my parents had taught me.

Then my husband reached his bottom and went to a treatment center. I enrolled in therapy groups that dealt with issues about being with an alcoholic spouse. In those groups, and in other counseling, therapist after therapist kept telling me I was an adult child of an alcoholic.

At first I couldn't accept that identification because I couldn't see any alcoholic drinking in my childhood. But through time, therapy, and a year of Al-Anon, I started to feel very ready to tackle adult children's issues. I was 36 years old.

I wasn't scared to attend my first ACOA meeting because of the familiarity I had with some of the terminology in therapy. I also felt very ready to do adult children's work. But at that first meeting, I cried for the entire hour and a half. For the first time in my life, I heard validation of all the feelings I had while I was growing up in my home. I had also had identification with the feelings I carried with me as an adult.

Never before had people understood me the way the adult children did. I remember when I was young talking to my friends and telling them how unhappy I was. But they saw my life from the outside and envied my wonderful family, my upper-middle class home, and my father who was respected by the peers in his profession.

In that one ACOA meeting, those feelings were finally understood and validated for me. It was scary at first, having total validation for a lifetime of feelings. I stayed away from ACOA for almost a month.

But during those four weeks, I thought about the things said at that first meeting. I had wanted to run out to my family of origin and share everything with them. I wanted to hear that they, too, felt the same way I did. I wanted those silences to finally be broken. My mind was working overtime, seeing for the first time how all the pieces of the puzzle were starting to fit together because of ACOA.

I started attending meetings regularly. I started talking about my feelings right away. But because of the lack of visible alcoholism in my family of origin, I still had a difficult time. I'd come home after hearing a speaker at the meeting talk about his alcoholic home and I'd think to myself, "Oh, my parents didn't really do all that to me."

I had difficulty with the lack of obvious alcoholism in my past. Some of the less-knowledgeable members of the ACOA group even told me people who didn't grow up with active alcoholism didn't belong in the group. That made me feel like an outsider all over again, just like I did when my sisters wouldn't include me in their fun.

However, through constant communication with solid, long-time members of the group, I kept going to the meetings. I kept sharing. And, over time and with reassurance, I began to feel I really belonged. I came to understand that the identifying symptoms of an adult child are the feelings, not the circumstances, of a person's childhood.

I went to my family and tried to talk to them about Adult Children of Alcoholics and some of the feelings I had. When I initiated a conversation with my parents, they started to open up at first. Then they got scared. They became angry and shut down. They now tell me they think the meetings are horrible.

I tried talking to my sisters. I really thought they would understand and start to share their feelings, because we all grew up in the same home and were certainly affected. One sister has been sporadically attending ACOA meetings on her own, but finds it difficult to acknowledge her feelings to herself and to me. My other sister identifies with the issues, but isn't ready to get involved with the program yet.

The denial on the part of my family really hurt at first. But since I've been going, I've learned that what's important to my growing in the program is the belief that recovery is really for me.

What can be . . .

My husband is also active in ACOA, and we share a lot. The meetings have proved to be enormously helpful in our family relationship with our two children.

I remember hearing parents share at one ACOA meeting about how difficult it was for them when their children started asking them what jealousy was, what love was, what feelings were. The parents had never really been taught about those emotions and were only just starting to be able to identify and feel them through their work in the program. My husband and I use the program to help us better express our feelings to our children.

We also benefit from the program in other areas besides feelings. Each of us has learned we have to take responsibility for ourselves, and we're now trying to teach our children to take responsibility for themselves. In the past, I played a martyr role with them. When they made a mess, I'd yell and scream and sigh, "Woe is me!" as I cleaned it up. They would, in turn, feel guilty.

Now if they spill something or make a mess, it's up to them to take responsibility for cleaning up. I don't do it for them. That way, they have a chance to make their own reparations. This helps them build their self-esteem.

My family is like a family now. We have the family meetings I'd always wanted to have while I was growing up. We communicate with each other by trying to talk feelings all the time. Even though we struggle and get angry and exhibit some adult children's behaviors from time to time, I can say our family life has improved enormously through my work in the program. I know now I'm a good parent. That means a great deal to me. But I also want to feel good about myself as a person. I want to learn how to enjoy doing things and how to accept achievements.

I guess in the beginning of my work in the program I thought I'd be a new person. I don't feel like one. Even though I still think life is painful, I know now if I allow myself to go through the pain and the feelings — the good as well as the bad — the rewards are tremendous. There is an inner peace awaiting me once I've worked through the feelings.

Today I feel like a person, rather than an alien from outer space looking in from the outside. I feel more like I'm part of the flow of things. I have a purpose and a right to be on this earth, and that helps me feel better about myself.

I'm going to constantly need the benefits of the ACOA program. In many ways I'm in my infancy in making changes. But what I have today is an ability to accept the present. I'm no longer looking for a Utopia in which to live. I'm no longer trying to please everyone by being a Miss Goody Two Shoes or a Perfect Parent or The Ultimate Human Being.

I have the ability now to look forward to a space where I'll be more comfortable with who I am. In that space, I'll be happy sometimes, sad sometimes, and even angry sometimes. But in that space, I will be a whole person. I will be me.

TIRED OF BEING ALONE

Dick's Story — Age: 50

It don't take much to see that something is wrong, but it does take some eyesight to see what will put it right again.

— Will Rogers

I grew up feeling a great deal of shame, fear, and anxiety. One of the causes of those feelings was my alcoholic father, who emotionally abused me. The other was my mother, a very controlling and possessive woman who sexually abused me when I was young.

As a child, and even as an adult, I always felt very alone and sad — as if I were out of step with the rest of the world. While I think part of me really wanted to have an active social life, another part of me felt incredibly insecure and incapable of having it. For years I struggled alone in an emotional depression. Then I found something that helped me through those times — prescription drugs. I started on a drug addiction that lasted over a decade, then began to drink heavily. My life was a mess.

I joined A.A. I discovered I was still carrying around some incredible feelings toward my deceased parents. I then sought counseling and the ACOA program. I started to share with others what it was like for me to grow up in my home.

I have become a different person today because of my decision to confront my past. I will never again have to face my childhood alone.

What once was . . .

I grew up in a cold-water flat with my parents and two older brothers. The older brother left for the war when I was five or six years old. The rest of us pretty much went our own way. If Mom discussed Pop with me at all, it was only to put him down. My parents never did anything together, and I never saw any physical interaction between them at all.

I don't ever remember a hug or a kiss or a conversation between my parents and me. There wasn't any give and take or sharing of ideas. I don't remember there being any sort of closeness or bonding in a natural sense.

In an unnatural sense, however, I did bond with my mother. Those memories are extremely painful to me, though I can remember only two episodes. Yet they haunted me throughout my adulthood and caused me incredible feelings of pain and shame. They began when I was between four and six years old.

I can see both of us lying in her bed, naked. She wanted me to play with her breasts and nipples. I was repulsed and felt sick inside. I refused to touch her, sensing there was something wrong with her request. She suggested I play with her earlobes. "That's what your brother likes to do," she said. I refused, but I knew I wasn't the only one she'd done this with. . . . It was cold in our flat. My mother had taken me to bed with her to "warm me up." We were naked. She wanted me to put my feet between her thighs so she could rub up against them.

Mom made me her husband in many ways, by the covert sexual activity as well as the things she chose to discuss with me and not with my father. As far back as I can recall, I can remember being concerned about money and finances and the electricity being shut off. Those were the types of things my mother would share with me, not "How was your day at school?" or "Do you want me to read to you?"

I hated being treated this way by my mother. I wanted to be far, far away from her, yet she totally controlled and possessed me in a very sick way. Even though I couldn't stand to be around her, I struggled to make sure I was near her. I felt guilty if I wasn't. For example, I remember one New Year's Eve when I was fourteen or fifteen years old. I was at a friend's house for a party. But right before the stroke of midnight I rushed back to my parent's house so I could be with them at the start of the new year. Then I raced back to the party.

I felt incredibly responsible for my parents despite their treatment of me. I felt it was up to me to make them feel better and to take care of them. I wanted to help them through their misery. All I wanted in return was a little recognition. But I never got it.

Pop was never there for me. He was mostly a weekend binge drinker, although I do have vague recollections of his being a daily drinker. During the week, he never missed a day's work. But on Saturday mornings he'd leave the house and come back drunk by two or three in the afternoon. He'd stay drunk or passed out all weekend.

It was awful when Pop drank. The alcohol made him mean. It literally changed his face. When he was sober he'd look like Pop, but when he was drinking he would look terribly evil. At those times, I thought he looked like the Devil. He also acted like the Devil in his biting, hurting comments toward me. His words etched incredible scars on me.

I felt so isolated in my house. I didn't feel a connection to anybody. I always felt very alone and very sad. I have no memories of warmth or love or caring or understanding. I only have memories of being alone and having to make it by myself. One time I burned my hands badly on steam, and I came home that night in a great deal of pain. But I didn't tell a soul what had happened. Instead, I drew a cool bath and sat in the water for a long time, letting my hands soak. After a while, someone yelled in to me, "Why are you staying in the bathtub so long?" I yelled back, "Because it feels good." I was left alone.

I think I didn't share my feelings with anyone for a couple of reasons. One was that I felt no one really cared anyway. My parents had never shown me that my feelings or anything I did really mattered. The other was I felt I was a lousy person. I grew up seeing myself as an undeserving, spoiled little brat. It wasn't that my parents gave me a lot of things or that I got my way a lot. I simply didn't feel valuable enough to ask for anything for myself, whether it be a motor scooter or a pat on the back. I had a really low opinion of myself and a great deal of shame for the kind of a person I believed I was.

No one seemed to notice my low self-esteem or my unwillingness to share my feelings. I don't believe anyone really noticed me. It was sad, but true: no one in the house noticed that it took me five years to graduate from high school instead of four. It was never questioned by anyone in the family. They just didn't seem to care.

I was not only alone in my house, I was also alone with my peers. I had no close friends. Then, when I was sixteen I met my wife, fell in love, and wanted to get married. I was tired of being alone. When I was twenty years old, we married.

A few short years later, I started going in and out of emotional depressions. They were hell, but I didn't share them with anyone. What I'd see in my mind was an image or picture of what the sexual abuse had looked like. It was almost like a photograph taken earlier, now developed and shown to me. Except I didn't get to pick the time or places I'd be shown the picture — it would just happen involuntarily. I could be walking down the street or just driving in my car, and suddenly the picture would be there.

As I saw the image, I'd start to feel guilty. I'd despise myself, knowing how rotten I was for seeing these images. I'd say to myself, "Look at you. You're a little down, a little depressed, and now you're picturing those things. What are you trying to do? Put the rap for your miserable feelings on your mother? What a miserable S.O.B. you are."

I endured those uncontrollable emotional downswings until I found something that took them away. That something was an injection of morphine I received from a doctor. I loved the morphine and the feelings I experienced with it. For the first time in my life, I felt at peace. I was 23 years old. From then until the age of 37, I pursued pharmaceutical drugs. When it became harder to legally obtain these drugs, I turned to booze. Within two or three years, I was a daily drinker.

During the time I was an active drug abuser, my mother died. I assumed total responsibility for Pop. And I mean total. He could do nothing for himself at that stage in his life. I became responsible for his life and care. Two years later, Pop died of a heart attack in the subway station. I remember to this day getting that phone call. The first thing I thought I felt was relief, and for years I carried an incredible amount of guilt because of that feeling. Later on, I discovered the feeling was one of release from him.

While my drug habits were escalating, so were some feelings that could be directly traced to my father's drinking behavior. I had some overwhelming feelings of anger. Whenever my wife and I argued or disagreed, I wanted to be abusive to her. It was almost as if I had a devil inside of me that I had to control or it would get control over me. While I was never physically abusive to her, I was verbally abusive in a way reminiscent of what my father had done to me.

I continued to hold the angry devil in check while feeling increasingly isolated from other people. I constantly abused alcohol and other drugs. I suffered my emotional downswings in silence.

Life, for me, was going rapidly downhill.

What is now . . .

In 1982, I got involved with A.A. Even though I stayed sober for the first two years, I was miserable. I knew there was something really wrong with me, but I didn't know what it was. The images of sexual abuse continued to march unannounced through my head.

But those times I'd react by saying, "Cut it out! Mom didn't do that to me!" I started remembering what it was like when Pop would yell at me when he was drunk and I'd say to myself, "Stop it! Pop didn't say those things to me!" I was becoming desperate to hold on to my denial of the past.

Little did I know my sobriety was in jeopardy. I just wasn't in touch with what was going on inside me. I went to a dentist one day for some dental work and asked for Percodans for the pain. I knew I wasn't asking for the physical pain, but for the emotional pain I was experiencing. I wanted to get high. But I knew something was wrong later when I filled the prescription and took twelve pills even though I had no pain at all. Then, I realized I would do anything to stop feeling the emotional pain.

After that incident, I decided to get help. I started seeing a therapist, went to a crisis intervention program at a treatment facility for three weeks, and began to deal with my adult child issues.

Interestingly enough, I had been to some Adult Children of Alcoholics meetings prior to my treatment. But in those meetings I hadn't dealt with the effect my parents had had upon me. Instead, I focused on my own children and started to look at the effect I was having on them. That fed right into my low self-esteem and guilt because I said to myself, "Look at what you've done to your daughters."

When I got out of the treatment facility, things started changing for the better. I learned alcoholism was a family disease, so my daughters and wife were encouraged to start therapy and go to their own meetings. Once my family started taking care of themselves, it was up to me to take care of myself. I had no choice, and that's exactly what I did. I even completed my Fourth and Fifth Steps, which I hadn't done in my two years in A.A.

I started attending ACOA regularly and focused on my feelings in the meetings. When I remembered how isolated I had felt growing up, I could look around me at all the people in the meeting and see I wasn't alone with those feelings. There were others who had gone through the same type of emotional and sexual abuse.

I was able to look at everything that had happened to me in a different light. Instead of blaming myself for everything and feeling shame, I could now say, "It wasn't your fault. There wasn't a thing you could've done about it. Now it's time to see the effect it's had on you, deal with it, and stop beating yourself up."

That's what I've been doing in ACOA.

What can be . . .

When I first started to recover in ACOA, I learned I didn't have to live my past anymore. I could still have feelings of anger toward my parents for the miserable childhood I had, but I didn't have to constantly relive the events of the past.

I used to say, "Mom and Pop did the best they could with the cards they were dealt in life." But it was that statement and the attitude that went along with it that kept me sick. I was defending their actions rather than stating, "Mom and Pop did the best they could — and it was a pretty rotten job. I've suffered as a result of it, and I need to work on getting myself better."

Once I was ready to let go of the past, it became easier to live in the present. I realized many of the fears I had as an adult could be directly traced to the emotional and sexual abuse I experienced as a child. To let go of that brought feelings of peace and a sense of release.

In the program, I realized that Mom's and Pop's death didn't mean my pain would go away. It just meant their abuse of me was over. Through ACOA, I've learned the program isn't about my parents, but about the effects my parents have had on me.

I'm not alone in those effects. There are many people who grew up in alcoholic homes. Each of these people is a mirror of myself, for I can see my pain in their eyes. With these mirrors, I've been able to see more than just my reflection. I've been able to see that I'm not alone.

Part of getting better is accepting the fact that it's okay to look at my needs and wants, especially my wants. I'm learning today to say, "I want this." I had never done that before because I never thought I deserved anything. My self-esteem is growing. I'm finally beginning to discover who Dick really is.

In a way, growing in the program is like shaving. I shave my face just about every day, but have I ever really looked at my face? Have I ever really seen what I look like? All I've really noticed is *what* I was shaving, not *who* I was shaving. But today that's changing and will continue to change. I hope someday to be able to look myself in the eyes and say, "You know, you really aren't such a bad guy. You really are pretty decent."

NOBODY LISTENED

Dee's Story — Age: 40

People are like children, they want so to be comforted and assured over and over again.

— Katherine H. Newcomb

I grew up the oldest of eight children in an alcoholic home. Yet not all of my problems were directly related to my mother's drinking and our protection of her. In fact, many of my issues were with my father and his treatment of two of my brothers.

The alcohol problem, combined with the size of the family, affected me in many ways for a good part of my life. Growing up, I always felt people weren't listening to me. I know I talked, I know I shared, but I really didn't believe anyone ever really heard me.

It wasn't until I started having some feelings of anger toward one of my own children that I started to reach my bottom. Surprisingly, it was my daughter's school counselor who gave me the key to dealing with some of the feelings I had had growing up in an alcoholic home.

But I finally hit bottom when my house was broken into and I was beaten. Suddenly I felt intense feelings of overprotection toward my mother, who I finally realized was an alcoholic. Once I started to deal with the reality of her disease, I was ready to deal with the reality of my issues as her adult child.

What once was . . .

My mother didn't start drinking heavily until I was in junior high school. But the years before that were far from peaceful, for I grew up in a household of seven brothers and sisters. The next oldest child was four years younger than I, but the rest of the siblings were spaced from a year and a half to two years apart. Needless to say, there was a great deal of confusion and constant activity in my house.

Yet I grew up feeling empty. I felt lost in the scope of the family. I felt overwhelmed by the tension that seemed to hum frequently around me. There were always a lot of people, a lot of noise, and a lot of motion in the house. The atmosphere of the house was not relaxing

159

while I was growing up. Within me at all times seemed to be an inner tension, a tight knot extending from my throat to my stomach.

Once my mother started drinking, things went from bad to worse. She would usually start drinking around four in the afternoon. I would have to come home right after school to baby-sit while she went over to her friend's house to drink. If they decided to drink at our house, I'd have to take the kids out of the house for a walk or something.

The drinking would last for a couple of hours. But by six o'clock, supper would be on the table as if there had been no interruptions in the normal flow of the household. My father would come home from work and walk in on an almost picture-perfect setting: the kids would be sitting around the table, steaming food would be waiting in bowls and on platters, and my mother would be sitting at the table.

Suppertime, though, was far from picture-perfect. I dreaded those meals because of all the tension. There was always a wait-until-Father-comes-home attitude that meant Father would handle any punishments or discussions while we were eating. I don't think there was a dinner where there wasn't the fear that someone would get slapped or even more than slapped. Two of my brothers in particular were my father's favorite targets. One of them was brilliant — probably gifted — but he couldn't function well in school. So there was always a great deal of discussion about the trouble he had gotten into at school.

I felt horrible inside, seeing those two brothers — or any member of my family — get beaten. I could hardly eat because my stomach would be in knots. My heart would ache for the child whose turn it was to get slapped or hit.

I spent years growing up trying to figure out why my father was so cruel and bitter toward us; then I gave up because I couldn't come up with any answers. He just seemed to be against us. It was almost as if my mother and the kids were his "victims." Even though he wasn't the alcoholic, we kids banded together as a unit against him. To us, he was the enemy.

No one thought of looking to our mother for support or protection at the times when our father abused any one of us. She'd be on her own, in her own blissful world, numb to the goings-on around her.

In truth, it seemed to me our mother and father didn't have any reality of what it meant to have children and be parents. As I grew older, I began to take on the responsibility I felt my parents should have. If one of them didn't attend a play or school function that a sister or brother was participating in, I'd feel badly and try to go to the function in my parents' place.

Sometimes I'd try to intercede and do some of the things I felt my parents should do to give them recognition for their achievements. Many times I became a parent to the children, telling them when to do things like get up on Sundays and go to church. As I look back now, I think I used guilt to get them to go because I felt the role model my parents was setting was so poor. But someone had to be responsible for the children. If my parents weren't going to do it, then I felt it was up to me to try and help out whenever I could.

Being from a large family meant I very rarely had any sense of individuality or freedom of choice. A good example of this were times when the whole family would go out for ice cream. That, in itself, would be quite a treat because a car filled with eight kids isn't the most welcome sight at a crowded ice cream stand, so we didn't go often.

As we parked the car, I'd be thinking about the flavor of ice cream I wanted, as would my brothers and sisters. One by one, we'd all yell out, "I want strawberry!" or "I want chocolate!" But my father would bellow back at us, "You're all getting vanilla!" And off he'd go to get eight vanilla ice cream cones.

The same thing would happen whenever there was the possibility of a choice or an expression of individuality. Rules and regulations were the same for everyone, as was the food put on the table for dinnertime — no matter how each person felt as an individual.

I grew up feeling lost. I felt I didn't exist.

I felt a great deal of sadness because of my mother's drinking. Rarely did I feel angry about it. Mostly I just felt sad and a bit embarrassed. I knew I shouldn't tell anyone about my mother's drinking.

When I got into high school I discovered that if I got involved with clubs and groups that met after school, I could get out of the baby-sitting responsibility and not come home until just before dinner was put on the table. So I tried out for sports, joined the student council — anything — just to get out of going directly home. If I didn't have responsibilities in organizations after school let out, I'd go over to a friend's house. Once I was old enough to get a part-time job, that was a big relief. That was one more way I had of staying away from the tension-filled, turmoil-ridden house.

Even though I stayed away from the house as much as possible, I knew my mother was still drinking. The times I still saw it firsthand were when our family would go on a vacation.

Because we were such a large family, we'd rarely go on a vacation together. Besides the expense, it was also extremely chaotic. But once in a while we'd try a vacation as a family, and the results weren't so great.

My mother loved the ocean. More than anything she'd choose times at the beach. One time she convinced my father to rent a cottage for a week near the ocean. She was ecstatic. "We're going to have a ball!" she exclaimed to us as the time neared for our departure. Since my father didn't share her enthusiasm for the beach, she invited her alcoholic sister for adult companionship.

Right from the start, my oldest cousin and I were put in charge of watching the kids while the two adults drank themselves into oblivion on the beach. Sometimes we'd have fun, all of us kids there with a big ocean to play in. But I didn't like being saddled with the responsibility of overseeing everyone.

One day, while we were all playing in the water and my mother and aunt were drinking, two kids got on a float and proceeded to drift quietly out to sea. I was in a panic. Although no disaster occurred, nobody seemed to notice how potentially dangerous the situation had been and how much responsibility they were giving me.

We didn't rent a cottage very often. Usually my mother and a drinking companion took us to the beach for the day. On the way home, they'd stop off at a bar for hours and leave us in the car. It would be hot, crowded, and boring. Every so often, they'd bring us out pop and bags of chips.

I lived at home while I was going to college. By that time my brothers and sisters were old enough to start communicating about what was going on around the house. Mostly we talked about how awful my father was. Rarely did we talk about my mother.

During the summers while I was in college I lived away from home, and I was so grateful to be free of the people and the tension. If I could describe what my inner feelings had looked like while I was growing up, I would say they were like a head of hair that's filled with numerous knots. In the tangled hair would be great big hands, trying to pull at all the knots. The feelings were of pain, of tension, and of turmoil.

I believed all of those tensions and pains would be behind me after I was married, and at first they seemed to be. When I had my first child, I thought that things couldn't be better. She was so easy to carry, easy to deliver, easy to take care of. She was total bliss, and I felt a great deal of love for her.

Then my son was born. He was not an easy baby from the start. After he was born, he was sick with colic. He was so difficult to take care of, for he was always crying and uncomfortable. My feelings toward him were the opposite of what I had felt for my daughter. She had given me a great sense of self-esteem. I saw how wonderful she was and how well-behaved and I thought, "I must be a wonderful mother. Look at the wonderful baby I have!" But with my son, I lost all my sense of self-esteem. I didn't believe I was really a good mother after all. I blamed myself for his behaviors and became extremely frustrated when nothing I did calmed him down or made him feel better.

I started to get very angry, almost feeling rage. After all those years growing up, when I felt so bad, I just wanted to start feeling good. My marriage was going sour, my daughter was being toilet trained, and my son was colicky. That's when I started to feel like I wanted to get rid of my anger as quickly as I could. My son was too tiny, but my daughter was getting older and bigger. I wanted to lash out at her. I felt lonely, helpless, and hopeless.

When my daughter was about six years old, a guidance counselor at a parents' open house night took me aside and told me my daughter was exhibiting some behavior signs that needed extra attention. I was told that children who need behavior modification may be bed wetters or stutterers, to name only a couple of signs. My daughter was a bed wetter.

The counselor suggested I do some behavior modification to help my daughter. I did the modification perfectly — so perfectly that I ended up with a perfect ex-bed wetter who started to suck her thumb.

I said to myself, "I think this isn't really the issue here."

What is now . . .

My marriage failed. I started going to a therapist and dealt with my family issues. I talked for quite a while with the therapist, mostly about my father. I rarely talked about my mother and her drinking problem.

Then, two and a half years ago, someone broke into my house and I was beaten. I hit bottom after that. I felt vulnerable, I cried a lot. Suddenly I became very worried about my mother being in her house without the kids around her for protection. I didn't feel safe as long as she was still drinking.

I helped draw the family together so we could do an intervention with my mother and get her into alcohol treatment. But there was still a great deal of denial about her drinking in the family, so I was left feeling as if I was the one with the problem. Nobody seemed to listen to me.

I didn't know where to turn for help. I think I was close to a nervous breakdown. I was crying a lot and felt very unsure of myself. I remembered hearing about Adult Children of Alcoholics, but I didn't make any moves to attend a meeting until I heard about an eight-week program on Adult Children of Alcoholics that was being offered by a local hospital. I signed up.

The program was run by a counselor and an adult child who was also in A.A. The sessions were mostly educational, showing films and talking about what an alcoholic family was like.

I couldn't believe the pain I felt after I left those sessions. I would leave in tears, not knowing what to do with the pain and sadness I was feeling. As the eight weeks neared an end, I was afraid of what I would do without those sessions to go to.

Luckily, I met a woman shortly after that who was in A.A. and in Adult Children of Alcoholics. She told me about a local meeting and gave me directions. As soon as I could, I went to that meeting on my own.

When I walked into the meeting, I was really scared. But it didn't take long before I felt like I had walked into the home I had always wanted. People were attentive to each other. They were really listening! They knew how I felt! There was no tension, no turmoil at the meeting. There was only caring and sharing.

I heard many new things at that meeting and at the ones I attended after that night. I heard I needed to learn how to put the focus on myself. All my life, my focus had been on other people. Even in my marriage, I had focused on my husband and tried to get him to talk about his feelings and share with me.

I learned there was a difference between self-caring and selfishness. Although I might have known what the definition of selfishness was, I don't think I ever really had heard about self-caring. Yet all around me were people who were learning how to nurture themselves. I wanted to learn — as fast as I could!

I remember how anxious I was the first night I attended an ACOA meeting. I remember I was at the lowest of lows in my life, when I discovered there were many, many things out of my control.

Those were the things that led me to Adult Children of Alcoholics. I have been grateful for the fact that I was led to ACOA. Sometimes I'm even happy I grew up in an alcoholic home, because now I've found a whole new way of life where people really listen.

What can be . . .

I've been in the program now for almost a year and a half. I'd like to say I'm "normal" now, but I don't know if I'll ever be able to say that.

I do have a sense of myself today that I never had before. I don't feel empty anymore. Even though I feel a little lost at times, I don't have that big, empty hole inside me that I once tried desperately to fill up.

I still feel sadness and even anger at times. But those emotions aren't as intense as they used to be because now I know I can do something about them. I don't have to live forever in sadness or anger. They are passing emotions — natural, yet not enduring.

I'm much more gentle today, both with myself and with other people. My relationship with my children has improved immensely since I've been working the program. Even though my son and I still have residual anger, it isn't as powerful and overwhelming as it used to be. I have a number of tools I can use today that calm me down so I don't reach that point of being out of control, in a rage.

But perhaps the greatest gift of the program is the return of my spirituality. When I was growing up, I was the one always pushing church onto my brothers and sisters as an obligation. I believed going to church was something that had to be done in order to be a good person. So I did countless good deeds in my effort to be a good person, like Sunday School and taking old people to church. But none of those things made me feel wonderful.

Now I do very few good deeds like those, but I feel so spiritual! I have so much more faith in the universe now and in the overall master plan. In the past I used to struggle to find the meaning of life and the reasons why for everything. Now I find I don't have to know. It's okay. I can just let things happen.

My life has meaning now. I am an individual and I can recognize myself as one. I have the freedom of choice in the program. I can decide what meetings I'll go to, what literature I'll read, what Steps I can study.

Today I don't have to have vanilla ice cream, for there's a whole world of flavors waiting for me to sample!

Hope for Adult Children of Alcoholics

These four cassettes record the workshop lectures and personal stories of some of the most respected speakers on adult children's issues today, including Earnie Larsen, Robert Subby and Barbara Naiditch. Individual tapes may be ordered separately.
Order No. 5629 Album of Four Cassettes

My House is Different
by Kathe DiGiovanni, M.A.

A beautiful storybook that interprets the Twelve Steps of recovery for children of alcoholics ages six through twelve. Joe and his dog Fuzzy travel down Rainbow Road and find a variety of creatures and adventures that help Joe learn how he can feel good about himself even if his dad continues to drink. (32 pp.)
Order No. 1387

Of Course You're Angry
by Gayle Rosellini and Mark Worden

Learning to express anger appropriately is difficult for families experiencing the escalated fear, guilt, and unpredictability in chemically dependent families. *Of Course You're Angry* offers specific guidelines for learning healthy ways to acknowledge and express our anger. (72 pp.)
Order No. 1169